HOPE THROUGH RECOVERY

WELBECK
BALANCE

ABOUT THE AUTHOR

Hope Virgo is a multi-award-winning mental health campaigner and advocate for people with eating disorders. Hope suffered with anorexia for over four years, before being admitted to a mental health hospital in 2007. She lived in the hospital for a year, fighting one of the hardest battles of her life. Her first book, *Stand Tall Little Girl* (Trigger Publishing, 2019), documents her harrowing, yet truly inspiring, journey.

Since being discharged, she has fought to stay well. Hope is now at the stage of "ongoing recovery" and uses her experiences of mental health illness to champion the rights of others, inspire them to get well, and help break the stigma of mental illness.

Hope is a recognized media spokesperson, having appeared on various platforms including *BBC Newsnight*, *Victoria Derbyshire*, *Good Morning Britain*, *Sky News*, *BBC Breakfast* and *BBC News*.

In 2018, Hope launched her #DumpTheScales campaign to ensure that nobody is turned away from treatment for eating disorders purely because of their weight. Hope has received cross-party governmental support for this, taken the petition to the UK Parliament, and continues to work with ministers to ensure that change is implemented.

HOPE THROUGH RECOVERY

YOUR GUIDE TO MOVING FORWARD
WHEN IN RECOVERY FROM AN
EATING DISORDER

HOPE VIRGO

WITH

DR CHI-CHI OBUAYA

WELBECK
BALANCE

A Trigger Book

Published by Welbeck Balance

An imprint of Welbeck Publishing Group

20 Mortimer Street

London W1T 3JW

First published by Welbeck Balance in 2021

ISBN

Trade Paperback – 9781789562569

Typeset by Lapiz Digital Services

Printed in Great Britain by CPI Group (UK) Ltd, Croydon CRO 4YY

10 9 8 7 6 5 4 3 2 1

Note/Disclaimer

Welbeck Balance encourages diversity and different viewpoints. However,
all views, thoughts, and opinions expressed in this book are the authors'
own and are not necessarily representative of Welbeck Publishing Group
as an organisation. All material in this book is set out in good faith
for general guidance; no liability can be accepted for loss or expense
incurred in following the information given. In particular, this book is not
intended to replace expert medical or psychiatric advice. It is intended for
informational purposes only and for your own personal use and guidance.
It is not intended to diagnose, treat or act as a substitute for professional
medical advice, and professional advice should be sought if desired before
embarking on any health-related programme.

www.welbeckpublishing.com

To all those who have battled the system to get support,
to those choosing to step forward in recovery each day, I know
how hard it can be when the battle is so loud in our heads,
but I also know how amazing it can be to feel yourself
winning at recovery.

And to my brothers and sisters, partner and friends,
who show so much patience and love when it comes to
my own wellbeing, you have all stood by me through a lot,
and continue to daily.

CONTENTS

Foreword   1
Introduction   3

Part 1: Living in Recovery   7
  1: My Story   9
  2: About Eating Disorders   25
  3: Where Are You Now?   37
  4: Ongoing Help   47
  5: Friends and Family   61
  6: Parenting Perspective   69

Part 2: Understanding Yourself   79
  7: Identifying Your Triggers   81
  8: Breaking the Habit of Counting   93
  9: Body Changes   103
  10: Your Mental Health   115
  11: Negotiating Diet Culture   123

Part 3: Daily Life   133
  12: School, University and Work   135
  13: Christmas   149
  14: Dinner Parties and Eating Out   155
  15: Exercise and Physical Activity   163
  16: Dating and Love   171
  17: Clothes Shopping   181
  18: Food Shopping   185
  19: Weddings   191

20: Holidays and Travelling   197
21: Dealing with Challenging Life Events   203

Part 4: Managing Relapse   213
22: About Relapse   215
23: Taking Action   225

Conclusion   233
Resources   239

FOREWORD

Join with computer audio – Check.

    Unmute – Check.

"Hello everyone..." As was the case with a number of professional conversations during the COVID-19 pandemic, my first meeting with Hope was in my capacity as a guest speaker on a Zoom lockdown webinar she was co-hosting. The meeting was one in a series of sessions to provide peer support to a range of people with eating disorders.

At the time, I fully recognized that Hope was an "expert by experience", something I value greatly within the mental health space. The sharing of these experiences has been an integral part of the drive to tackle the stigma associated with mental ill-health in recent years. While, in general, I am not of the opinion that you have to have experienced a given psychiatric disorder to treat a patient with care and empathy as a professional, with respect to eating disorders (alongside drug and alcohol addictions, in particular), there is a unique perspective that comes from hearing about the lived experience of someone in recovery.

I was familiar with Hope's activism and her reputation as an outspoken advocate for people with eating disorders, but I felt a degree of trepidation as I prepared to join the webinar. Little did I know that a few months later we would be collaborating on *Hope Through Recovery*!

My personal experience has been that the relationship between psychiatrists and people who have been in contact with eating disorders services can be challenging and combative. I certainly wondered what Hope thought of the psychiatrists she had come across and thus what she would make of me. Would I be cast as an ally or the enemy? At the same time, I hoped that she would offer sound advice to the webinar participants that would not sit at odds with my own suggestions.

As with the webinar, I found reading *Hope Through Recovery* engaging, insightful and thought-provoking. And I hope all readers will find it encouraging and benefit from its tangible, practical takeaways. Grounded in lived experience, this book will undoubtedly inspire and hearten those walking a path Hope has trodden. She packs no punches and has been brave enough to share many deeply personal memories that have marked her journey; I commend her immensely for doing so.

Hope Through Recovery courageously and expertly sheds light on a broad range of issues, such as the frustration of dealing with healthcare professionals that don't seem to "get it" and navigating intimate relationships when your body image is diminished. You will also encounter a treasure trove of practical tips, from managing workplace lunches to wedding planning when you have an eating disorder.

Whether you are at the start of your recovery or have been in recovery for some time, whatever your starting point is, as you delve into Hope's book, there is a plethora of relatable material to reflect on. I encourage you to immerse yourself fully in Hope's world as you journey with her.

Dr Chi-Chi Obuaya
October 2020

INTRODUCTION

In September 2008, I was discharged from the Riverside Mental Health Hospital where I had spent a year in recovery from anorexia. Despite looking like a completely new woman on the outside – a healthy weight, a glow back in my face, fuller hair – the reality was that my recovery was far from finished.

There is no denying that the hospital had saved my life and given me amazing care, but I was extremely institutionalized. I had no idea how to live in the real world. How was I ever going to live normally? What would I do if I went to a restaurant? How would I know what to eat each day without following my calorie-controlled diet? What would happen when I started living on my own? How would I cope with life's challenges, such as relationship break-ups and the loss of loved ones?

This book is the one I needed back then, answering all these questions and more, and helping me to face the fears that stopped me living my life fully in recovery.

Where are you in your recovery? Maybe you have just left hospital or are taking that step to end treatment... maybe you have battled your whole life, but never had a formal diagnosis or got the help you deserve... or maybe you are functioning in recovery. Perhaps you have been given this book and are reading it thinking it isn't relevant to you, that no one really understands what you are going through. You may be unsure if recovery is something that is for you...

Whatever your stage of recovery, this book can play a part with the guidance, reassurance and practical advice it offers. Try to be open-minded to the content and talk about it to those in your support network who you trust. Know that it is written by someone who has been through recovery and relapse and recovery again, and has battled the system along the way. Someone whose whole identity was tied up in eating disorders and who was convinced that anorexia would make everything okay… who believed that eating and acknowledging feelings meant losing control. Someone who was fearful of accepting help and starting on the road to recovery, but who is now sitting here 12 years later and can tell you that the long, hard journey was worth it.

I hope that by sharing my story – and the stories of others – it will inspire and equip you to tackle your recovery head on. Remember, you are not alone in this.

How to Use this Book

This book isn't meant to be read all in one go (although, of course, you can do that if you wish). Use it as a handbook, which you can dip in and out of. Make notes, talk to people while you read it, and question the bits you want more clarity over.

The exercises you'll find in each chapter aren't designed to be easy – some of them will feel really tough – but hopefully they will help you take a few more steps forward. Take your time over doing the exercises and go back to them when you need to, so you can get really into them and build your confidence.

There are tips throughout, and I have written this book with the help of Consultant Psychiatrist Dr Chi-Chi Obuaya, who offers additional insight into the methods I suggest, and uses his years of experience to impart invaluable advice.

PART 1: LIVING IN RECOVERY

In this part you can read my own story to give you a sense of the journey I've been on and why I want to use that to help others. You'll gain a clear understanding of eating disorders as a mental health disorder, and what you might be up against in terms of getting the help you need. There are exercises to assess where you are in your recovery and help you move forward. All aspects of support are included, from medical services to therapy to the support of friends and family, and Part 1 ends with a chapter aimed at parents and carers of someone with an eating disorder.

PART 2: UNDERSTANDING YOURSELF

This part explores how habits form and how to break them, and helps you identify your individual triggers and navigate society's negative diet culture. There's a chapter on body image that gives you coping strategies for those days when how you feel about your body might trigger you and a wider look at the mental health issues that affect wellbeing. All of the things learned in this section can be taken forward as we look at everyday life in Part 3.

PART 3: DAILY LIFE

This parts helps you to navigate everyday life while you are in recovery. There are exercises and advice to help you function at work or in education, enjoy going out for dinner and socializing, cope with big events such as Christmas and weddings, and take some of the stress out of food shopping and clothes shopping. I look at how to make exercise a healthy part of your recovery and show you how it is possible to make holidays and travel part of your recovery journey.

PART 4: MANAGING RELAPSE

In this part we look at the possible stages of relapse and how to spot the warning signs. There are exercises to help you make a clear plan of action to get the help you need and take care of yourself.

PART 1
LIVING IN RECOVERY

CHAPTER 1

MY STORY

Growing up, I had always struggled with my emotions. I felt different from people around me, including the rest of my family, but could never really pinpoint why. When aged nine, I was sent to see a therapist, but nothing really changed for me. I went to see her week after week for about six months and sat there trying to work out what to say, what answers to give. I just didn't get why people had to talk about their emotions. What was so important about that? I had ways of dealing with things that worked for me – my main tactic was avoidance. I hated feeling anything and longed to switch off my emotions.

The therapist, a bit of a hippy, worked from her big house in Bristol. I remember the therapy room having two big tables and some sofas. She would ask me to write my bad habits down on pieces of paper and put them into an empty tissue box. I would just stare at the box. I couldn't think of what to write. I pretended that I bit my nails as I had heard people say how gross that was. Throughout the session we would move our way around each area, talking, painting and writing. One week she got annoyed because I used my paintbrush in different colours for a picture. I was shocked that she got cross with me. It seemed that even in therapy, a supposedly safe place, I couldn't even get it right. I didn't feel heard and I definitely didn't feel safe. Back then I kept telling myself it was okay – if I held it together, it would be easier. Anything to keep the peace at home, and in my brain. And when the therapy finally came to an end, the reality was I still struggled with my emotions, but maybe it wasn't so bad to be like that, maybe that was okay. I convinced myself it was fine. Life was fine; everything was fine! And the more I told myself that, the easier it became to mask those feelings. I felt able to put on a front and push those emotions further and further down. Little did I know that this was going to be a continuing theme in my life – pretending things were okay and hiding who I really was.

By the time I joined senior school, I was feeling unhappier and quite lost and alone a lot of the time. My family were arguing a lot and I was constantly trying to find ways to distract myself from everything going on around me. Around that time, I was also sexually abused. It started quite slowly, being sucked in to someone's life. He emailed me every day, telling me that my family were all nasty. He gradually pulled me closer and for some reason I felt able to trust him. I would email him after I had argued with my parents or after a bad day at school. After months of corresponding, he would turn up on my walk home from school. He would become frustrated if I was with my friends and as I was afraid of upsetting him, I would make my excuses and leave my friends to walk back with him. The relationship gradually became more physical and over the next eight months he made me do things to him that I didn't understand. He explored my body and it hurt. I felt so trapped. After the first time, he told me not to tell anyone as they would get annoyed with us and try to stop this "love". So I kept quiet, but the more it progressed the more trapped I felt. I was carrying this constant guilt around with me and feeling so afraid. I hated how it made me feel, but didn't know where to go or who to talk to.

One day he pulled over in a quiet road after dropping everyone off from a church service first. I was sitting there feeling a bit stuck. I had been so desperate for him to drop me earlier in the journey, each week praying hard that he would, but he never did. He turned off the engine and reached over to me. He undid his trousers and pulled my head over him, pushing it deeper into his groin. I felt disgusted at him and at myself, and so angry with God. To block out what was happening, I thought about shopping with my friends, about the schoolwork that I needed to do, and then I started to think about food.

A Turning Point

It was at that point on that Sunday evening that my life changed again, and the lies and deceit escalated. My relationship with food continued to change slowly over the next few weeks and months. A voice in my head told me that if I skipped a meal, or thought about calories, it would help to take me away from those horrible feelings and give me some sense of control over my life.

I loved the distraction it gave me – the distraction from the abuse as his hands wandered over my body, or when they reached for me in places I didn't even know existed, causing pain to shoot through me. The upset and guilt that followed those episodes was so excruciating that I needed to find a way to deal with it. And that's what anorexia gave me. It became my beautiful, wonderful best friend; reassuring me when no one else could, loving me when I felt so alone, and helping to take away all that pain.

The anorexia was constantly with me, constantly reassuring me. It gave me this real value and sense of purpose, helping to numb all my emotions every day. It gave me a sense of control over my life and helped me escape the reality of growing up. I loved how it made me feel for those first few years as the "friendship" developed. I loved that I could watch my family argue and watch my abuser tell me what to do, and feel nothing! My fake plastered smile hid everything that was going on inside me.

There were points when I hated it, but for those first few years anorexia kept me alive and safe. Little did I know that what I was doing was dangerous and that this "love affair" would soon turn toxic.

After about three years of trudging along with this voice in my head, the happiness began subsiding. When I didn't do exactly what the voice told me to do – eat exactly the right amount of food – I was left with intense feelings of guilt. I blamed myself. I needed to up my game! Anorexia pushed me and pushed me each day; and even though some days I messed up, I knew that when I did listen I would get rewarded. I thought I had found this magical solution to life. This solution to pain, anger and emotion. Each day, I longed for more of it. From feeling nothing and numbing my emotions to gaining control, I realized that I needed to do more to satisfy the anorexia.

It became easy to hide what was happening from everyone. I learned how to shut down conversations and cause big family arguments to avoid eating. I was constantly out and about at sports practices. Even at school it became easy to hide food at lunchtime or to plan activities to avoid mealtimes. But over this period of my life things were getting harder. I was running out of energy, I was tired and while I was enjoying hiding my feelings and emotions, it still wasn't enough. Each day I wanted to push myself further and further, but it was getting harder and my brain was so tired by the same cycle every day. A lot of the time I hated that voice inside my head; the way it controlled me and made me feel. But I felt like there was no way out. I was totally trapped.

Under the Spotlight

Fast forward four years from when I first sat in that car thinking about food and my whole life began to get scrutinized. After the summer of my GCSEs, my school picked up on my weight change. They contacted my parents and asked them to take me to the doctor, who ran some tests on my thyroid. Looking back, it is pretty ridiculous that it took so long to get a diagnosis and a referral, but at the time I loved the delay. Finally, I was referred to Child and Adolescent Mental Health Services (CAMHs) and attended a mid-week appointment with my mum. I remember walking into a massive hospital with huge, high ceilings – and as we walked along I felt so nervous. I didn't really understand why I was there and thought the whole thing was a bit of a waste of time. Like come on, I could be out there exercising, but instead I am sitting in a waiting room. I was trying to take it all in – posters on the wall about "OCD", "Depression", "Eating Disorders". The words jumped out at me from the notice board and I kept thinking to myself, "Why am I here? Am I just going to get labelled?" I had Googled some of this stuff, but only for interest – I didn't really think it applied to me.

"Jennifer Hope Virgo"; my name was called out and it pierced through the silence of the room, echoing down the corridors. I followed the man who had called my name. He had a friendly face, but I still felt reserved. I wasn't sure what was really going on. I thought back to the times when I had been in that therapy room when I was nine, when nothing was really explained to me. I knew I had to pull myself together, put up my guard, and not let anyone in. That was what would get me through the next hour.

I sat down in a chair in the office, with my mum seated beside me. The therapist asked me what I thought I was doing there, and when I didn't really answer he moved on to talk to my mum. She talked about my history, my past therapy, my family dynamics … it went on and on! I wasn't entirely sure what to make of the therapist, or this whole situation. Occasionally, my eyes would dart around the room, looking at the notices on the board, and the "thank you" cards on the desk.

At the end of that appointment I was introduced to another therapist, who sat opposite me while I completed various questionnaires. I sat there staring at the bits of paper in front of me, with questions about my feelings and my emotions. Asking about my relationships with other people and with food. I looked down at it all, just staring and trying to work out what I should write and how honest I wanted to be.

I left the appointment still feeling completely lost. My mum was beginning to watch my every move and it was frustrating me. I didn't understand why suddenly people felt the need to interfere – I had been hurting for so long and had found my own solution to pain.

At my second appointment I was diagnosed with anorexia. The hospital sent pages and pages about me, detailing where I was on the charts and all the information they had collated from my family. That evening I Googled anorexia and ended up down a rabbit hole. In the past I had looked at diet hashtags, and hashtags promoting thin ideals, but had never really gotten deeply into it. Despite being in denial about having anorexia, I could see some similar traits to other people online, but I felt no way like them. I wasn't thin for a start and I liked food.

Over the next few months I continued at CAMHs, each week lying and putting on that mask.

Health Concerns

It was November 2007 when my life took another change. I was sitting in a waiting room at the front of an inpatient mental health adolescent hospital in Bristol, with my parents either side of me. All of us were quite anxious and a bit on edge. My dad kept standing up, which infuriated me. Couldn't he just sit down? My mum looked over at me every now and then, telling me it was going to be okay. But was it? I had no idea what was about to happen.

The last 24 hours hung over us. My ECG results had come back showing that my heart was likely to stop at any moment. I had been out at the time, walking with my older brother, shopping for clothes for him. Mum had phoned to say we had to come straight home. I went for a blood test immediately, and that was followed by a huge family argument about what was right for me. I guess the reality was that those arguments had pretty much been my life for the last year or so. They didn't bother me anymore. Instead, I just stood and listened. Arguments were the norm ever since my parents had decided to interfere with my eating and made me go to CAMHs.

As I sat in the hot waiting room, my mind wandered – I thought about exercising, about how I was going to avoid eating after this meeting, when we would inevitably go out for a coffee and my parents would sit awkwardly opposite me watching to see what I would eat. I didn't really know why I was sat there. I was angry that they were interfering; it wasn't anything to do with them. The door opened and we were taken into the family therapy room.

There were three members of staff on one side of the room and my parents and me on the other. I sat there fidgeting. I didn't care that I was being rude and impatient. I wanted everyone to know that I didn't want to be there. The meeting was all a bit of a blur. Words like thin, dead and emaciated were flung round freely. And then I was whisked off to get weighed.

As I arrived in the hospital that day, little did I know that I would be back in there 24 hours later, about to take on the biggest challenge of my life.

We went over my diagnosis from the previous hospital, and after lots of discussions and a sea of tension between my parents, they told me that I had no choice but to return there the next day.

I sat in silence next to my mum on the way home from the hospital. When I got home, I went straight up to my room and started putting empty sick bags, empty diet coke bottles, calorie books, and scales into a bin bag. I looked around my room – the vomit stain on the carpet, the bin I had once loved, made out of an empty chocolate Heroes tin, covered in vomit stains. I looked in the mirror, pulling apart my stomach. I texted all my friends and said I wouldn't be back in school tomorrow so could we go for dinner. Seriously, what a question! As I was leaving the house that evening my mum suggested I ate something at home before I left, but what was the point. I lied, telling her I would eat with my friends, both of us knowing that I wouldn't bother.

As I got into bed that evening, I didn't feel anything. Maybe I was in denial about the hospital admission, or maybe I didn't think it was actually going to happen. Maybe I was relieved that someone was taking away any choice I had about food.

My Hospital Admission

As I stood there in the entrance to the hospital on my admission day, the anger rushed away from me. My mask disappeared – that cold face that had been there for so long – and I was filled with the emotions I had bottled up for months, maybe even years. I was absolutely terrified. I begged my mum to let me come home and promised her I would eat and do what she wanted, but she refused. I hated her at that moment; I hated her for leaving me there. I felt like everyone was giving up on me.

I had arrived at 10.30 am, had a quick chat with a nurse, and put my bags in my bedroom. At 11 am it was snack time. This made me even angrier. Why did they get me in for this? I struggled my way through a milky protein drink, the cold sweat dripping down my back. I looked around the room where we were all sitting. There were nurses eating biscuits and drinking coffee, and the other eating disorder patients looking at me shiftily. They introduced me to two girls who were in my room. I kept trying to concentrate on other things to avoid drinking, while this nurse kept nudging me. It was infuriating and quite embarrassing. Maybe that is what they would do… shame me into eating. I was sent to rest until lunchtime. As I lay there in bed wishing I was working out instead, I thought back to the last few months. They had been a complete muddle and a mess.

I would get up in the morning, sneak off to the gym or go for a run before school. I was finding new ways daily to skip meals. I'd sneak out of school to work out as early as I could. My mind was elsewhere thinking about calories, exercise, how I could avoid the next meal, or where I could hide food to pretend I had eaten it. I was disengaged with school and my friends. I didn't know what my friends and teachers thought of me, but I didn't really care at this point. My evenings would be spent exercising, causing a family row to avoid eating, or forcing down a meal followed by hours of vomiting in the bathroom. I would crawl into bed in the early hours of the morning smelling of vomit and sweat, wishing my life was over. Wishing I would never wake up.

The week before I had shouted at my dad for making me eat and to get back at him, I had stood there stuffing dry bread into my mouth. My dad's eyes had filled with tears, but I didn't care. As I left the room after shuffling a few bits of bread into my mouth, I shouted, "I hate you. I hope this makes you happy," while launching the bread across the room.

The anorexia had turned me into a nasty, selfish person.

The evening when I had shouted at my dad, I thought it was okay to eat the bread as I would be able to make myself sick. However, as I dashed up the stairs all the bathrooms were taken. How was this possible? I had no choice... I went into my bedroom, turned off the light to pretend I was going to sleep, and I vomited into my pillowcase. The smell of vomit consumed me, my bedroom, and all my bedding. I had two doors in my bedroom at either end, and as I glanced between the two of them I kept purging. I knew I had to, that if I didn't, the guilt would just be too much.

So, this is where I was now. Stuck in a hospital, aged 17, with my life completely on hold and with so much uncertainty about what was going to happen. There was so much anger inside me, so much pain.

The thing with eating disorders and our culture today is that we praise weight loss, so when I arrived in hospital and found out I had to start putting on weight I didn't get it. Why me? People kept pushing the word anorexia, but I didn't think it was a thing. And I definitely didn't think I had anything the matter with me.

Eating disorders are so powerful — we believe that if we "listen" to them, we will feel okay! They make us feel totally invincible and, like me, you may not have realized how dangerous they are. You may be reading this because you have been told to, or you may be thinking but Hope I am older, I have kids already, I have a job... and, yes, I get it. Many people do function at a high level with an eating disorder, but you probably aren't that happy. I hate to be so blunt, but you might be just plodding along. I know I was for so long. I convinced myself I was happy and I really wasn't. Outside I looked it, but inside that was far from the truth.

On the Friday night, after being in hospital for three days, I felt completely fed up. I hated that all my friends were out enjoying themselves and I was trapped in here. That evening Emma, one of the nurses, came in with some massive pieces of brown paper. After marking my head and feet on one piece of paper, she asked me to draw an outline of my body. She then asked me to lie down on the same piece of paper and she traced around me. I stood up and looked at the images. Two images that were so, so different. I thought she had somehow tricked me, but then realized that the way I viewed myself was so distorted. I was overwhelmed with emotion as I stood staring down at the drawing, but I kept trying to push those emotions further and further away. I was confused and felt so alone and frightened, but that Friday night, doing that drawing exercise gave me what I needed to start taking steps forward in my recovery. It wasn't plain sailing from then on, but it helped me start to accept that something was the matter and that I needed to start eating. Despite the ECG and bloods results, I had longed for evidence for so long and this was the evidence that helped!

Learning to Open Up

A year of hospital treatment was hard work and intense, but it helped. I learned the importance of eating. I learned why I wanted to stay well, and I taught myself the power of engaging with my emotions and talking about how I feel. Yes, the talking is something that I still find hard, but I know how much it helps.

It is hard work to cross over to the other side of recovery, but I can promise you that it is so, so possible! Being in hospital allowed me to realize all of the stuff that I wanted to do, from going to university, to having a fresh start, to being able to go out with friends for food.

We use our eating disorder to numb our feelings, to perhaps hide something that we have been through, so when we start to recover, the feelings that we hid for so long start to surface. This inevitably means we have to tackle what is going on and if we don't, those things will resurface. I had a huge range of therapy during my hospital admission, but I want to mention the two types that really worked for me. The first one was the face-to-face talking therapy because it gave me the space to be heard. The other one that I found really helpful was the eating disorder group after mealtimes. We ate our meals and were often left with so many different feelings of guilt, failure and disgust. This group gave us the chance to share and talk about those feelings. It felt so uncomfortable at first and so hard to air what was going on in my head, but the more we did it the easier it felt. It was those groups that so often got me through the mealtimes.

Don't get me wrong – at first it was so hard, but as I began to open up things got easier. It felt so uncomfortable at times, not least because when you stop starving yourself your feelings and emotions come back with a vengeance. But the more I pushed through it, the easier it got.

Further Challenges

I was discharged in 2008 after a year and while there is no doubt that the hospital saved my life, I was presented with challenges over the next 11 years that pushed my recovery to its limits. Things that I came up against in work, in day-to-day life, and in various difficult circumstances. Life felt really hard at times, but what I learned through it all was the more we keep going and the more we fight onwards, the better it is.

I am here now in 2020 and thriving (even though I find that word quite cringeful!). I don't let the eating disorder stop me doing things; it doesn't control my day-to-day life. Yes, recovery might feel uncomfortable at times – right now it might actually feel absolutely terrifying for you – but when we challenge it and push it out, it gets easier!

Since leaving hospital I have made so much progress in my recovery and am constantly pushing myself further and further. I have learned to listen to myself and what my brain needs. Along the way I have learned the things that work for me and the things that have helped me push myself further. I am not going to paint this happy-clappy picture of recovery, but it does get easier, and it can be amazing. Hold on to this truth as you read the book, be open-minded and always question yourself.

THINGS THAT HELPED ME IN RECOVERY

Physical activity: I am aware it is controversial to state that exercising aided my recovery, but I believe that moving into a space where you can exercise in a healthy way is okay and important.

Knowing my triggers: We all have triggers in life, whether we have had an eating disorder or not, and it is important to identify what they are so that we can respond in a safe way.

Challenging myself: This started after about eight years into my recovery. I realized I spent a lot of my time functioning. I ate the same food a lot of the time, had the same drinks, went to the same restaurants... I realized that although I felt mostly okay, there was still something holding me back. So, I decided to stop and commit to challenging my recovery every day – for example, I would push myself to eat a different snack, try a new restaurant or order something I actually wanted off a menu! It felt hard at times, but the more I did it the easier it got, and the more I was able to push myself into a better space in my recovery.

Being mindful of social media: I took ownership of what I looked at, limited my time, and became aware of the things that left me feeling worse.

Tackling mealtimes: Making sure mealtimes are enjoyable and that there are no negative emotions associated with them. For me this included not receiving bad news at mealtimes, or in the surrounding hour, not having arguments during mealtimes and making sure that any unresolved issues were addressed before we ate. Keeping mealtimes neutral and safe has been an important part of my recovery as it stops me feeling the need to express myself using food.

Journalling: I write a lot, about everything! Getting all my feelings down on paper really helps with rumination and to make sense of things.

Booking trips: Travelling was a huge motivator for me in hospital. Having the space to travel and have things I am looking forward to really helps.

Therapy: Over my recovery journey, I have done different amounts and types of therapy, but just having that space to feel heard always helps. Therapy can be life-changing and help you to learn so much about yourself.

Communicating with others: It really helps.

Knowing My Triggers

Throughout your journey, you will discover what works for you and heal at your own pace. People may try to derail you, but when they do, make sure you keep pushing yourself further ahead.

Remember, it isn't selfish to focus on your own wellbeing. The truth is, it won't be easy, but it is so worth pushing yourself and accepting that you will have ups and downs. When we have difficult times, we need to be aware of how long they go on for and if we need more serious support.

Things have been really hard for me twice since coming out of hospital: one was my relapse in 2016 (see Part 4) and the other in 2019 when I had finished my sexual abuse case. In 2019 things had felt hard, I had spent a while reliving the sexual abuse through various police interviews, but hadn't realized the long-term impact this had on me. Overall, life got really tough, but I hid it for so long and tried to manage it. I hated so much of life, grew to resent everything around me, and I felt completely trapped. But I convinced myself that everything was okay. That life would and could just be amazing if I worked harder at my job. What I missed was noticing those triggers, the things that should have been the warning signs.

Below are a few of my warning signs... I wonder what would be on your list?

1   I was a workaholic.
2   I tried to please too many people.
3   I let people get to me.
4   I focused on fixing others rather than embracing my feelings.
5   Reporting the sexual abuse.

In September 2018, I reported being sexually abused as a child – it was a massive thing for me to do. It was so hard, having boxed something up for that long, to release it into the world. I thought I was strong enough for no professional support at the time, but the flashbacks should have been a warning sign. Instead, I let it get the better of me and as my guard built up to protect me, again I hurt those closest to me.

At first I felt myself slipping into that pit of self-blame. I hated my brain in that moment; I hated that I lost so much to my past, but I knew there was no point stressing about it now, no point in wallowing in self-pity. I knew I had a choice to make (incidentally, we always have a choice, though it may not always feel that way!).

I remember it so vividly. It was June 2018; I was sitting at King's Cross Station, in between meetings, crying, not entirely sure what to do with myself. I wasn't suicidal, but I was just so broken. Friends had been telling me for weeks to get support, but I hadn't listened. Something in me that day helped me realize I needed to tackle this and that I had to act fast.

The thing is, having these moments of realization does not make us weak, nor does having bad days in recovery. It is about how we deal with those days.

What do you do on those days when life feels really hard? What do you do when that part of your brain is nagging you, trying so hard to suck you back in?

I really hope that this book can help empower you to deal with those days in the right way, help you to talk, open up, and to know that you can and will get through this.

CHAPTER 2

ABOUT EATING DISORDERS

If I ask you to think of someone with an eating disorder, what springs to mind?

Most likely, it will be the image of an anorexic, white teenage girl, looking gaunt, extremely skeletal with maybe a yellowish tint to her skin. Does it shock you to know that out of the 1.6 million people currently diagnosed with an eating disorder in the UK, only 8% have anorexia?[1] This statistic certainly shocked me. I thought for so long that people with eating disorders were predominately living with anorexia. Even though there are so many other types of eating disorders, we tend to judge the severity of one by how thin someone is. A high percentage of people do not have the "well-known" eating disorders, nor may they "look" like they have an eating disorder.

We need to make sure *everyone* feels listened to and realize that it's not only about weight or physical appearance: an eating disorder is a *mental* illness.

The NHS describes an eating disorder as having: "an unhealthy attitude to food, which can take over your life and make you ill. It can involve eating too much or too little, or becoming obsessed with your weight and body shape."[2]

---

1   Hay *et al* (2015). Current approach to eating disorders. *Internal Medicine Journal*, 50(1), pp. 24–29.

2   NICE guideline NG69 (2017). Eating disorders: recognition and treatment. Available at: www.nice.org.uk/guidance/ng69/chapter/Recommendations

EATING DISORDERS STATISTICS (UK)

- 1.6 million people in the UK struggle with an eating disorder.
- On an annual basis, eating disorders cost the health service £80–100 million and cost the economy more than £1.26 billion annually.
- 8% have anorexia, 19% have bulimia, 23% have a binge eating disorder; 50% have other specified feeding disorders.[3]

There are many different types of eating disorders, and each person who develops one will have their own unique story around it. Specific eating disorders include anorexia nervosa, bulimia nervosa, binge eating disorder, diabulimia and pica. It is important to remember that while these conditions are about eating behaviours, there is so much more to them than food. Eating disorders aren't about dieting, or about being a certain size. They are about being in control and numbing emotions; they are a coping mechanism to help someone get through life's difficulties.

DEFINITIONS OF EATING DISORDERS... FROM DR OBUAYA

The diagnostic criteria for anorexia nervosa is:

- Maintained body weight of at least 15% below that expected for the height of individual, i.e. a BMI under 17.5 (weight in kilograms divided by height in metres squared)
- Morbid "fear of fatness"

---

3 Hay et al (2015). Current approach to eating disorders. *Internal Medicine Journal*, 50(1), pp. 24–29.

- Distorted body image/self-esteem unduly influenced by weight and shape
- Weight loss self-induced by voluntary avoidance of food and also sometimes other weight losing methods such as self-induced vomiting, purging, excessive exercise or use of appetite suppressant drugs or diuretics
- Amenorrhoea (absence of menstrual period) for over three months.[4]

The major international diagnostic manuals used by psychiatrists to diagnose mental health conditions (ICD-10 and DSM-5) recognize a number of other eating disorders, including:

- 'Eating Disorder Not Otherwise Specified' (EDNOS in ICD-10), also known as Other Specified Feeding and Eating Disorders (OSFED in DSM-5) – this can consist of the core symptoms of anorexia occurring at a 'normal' weight
- Avoidant/Restrictive Food Intake Disorder (ARFID), in which there is reduced food intake or range but no body weight/shape concerns and no anorexic cognitions; may be associated with vomiting phobia and is linked to Autism Spectrum Disorder (ASD)
- 'Orthorexia' is a term used to describe a preoccupation with 'pure' or 'clean' eating.

Remember, eating disorder treatment is not about just feeding someone or getting them to accept a specific diet. It is about treating a mental illness.

---

4   World Health Organization (1992). *The ICD-10 Classification of Mental & Behavioural Disorders.* **Geneva: World Health Organization.**

Barriers to Treatment

I believe that society has developed in such a way so that disordered eating has become the norm. We are bombarded with messages daily suggesting that in order to be happy we need to be "thinner", or if we lose weight people compliment it. There is a huge focus on diet culture, food challenges, and the messaging pushed out across the country that a high number of people struggle with disordered eating. People with eating disorders cross over into the serious end of this spectrum but I felt it necessary to draw this in because I know for a lot of you reading this, you might have friends or family members who have a disordered relationship with food which can make recovery feel much harder.

This is extremely dangerous and makes it hard for many people to get the support they need.

Eating disorders are treated differently around the world; some cultures hide a person away, some charge excessive amounts of money for treatment, while others try to offer support but struggle with huge funding issues. Don't worry, this isn't a political book, but I want to highlight the different approaches to treatment. That's because struggling to get support once you've decided to try and then being turned away feels *terrible*.

I know how it feels to ask for support only to be told you aren't thin enough. Perhaps this happened to you, perhaps you have tried to access treatment but weren't able to. Maybe you tried so hard, but as soon as you were turned away, the eating disorder kicked in telling you that you didn't deserve help anyway. I've also met people who feel like failures because they aren't underweight enough to qualify for help. If this is you, there are things you can do if you find yourself in this position.

While a lot of you will have picked up this book because you are leaving treatment, I know there will be some of you who haven't actually managed to get treatment. Not because you don't deserve it, but because the system won't allow you to get support.

No matter what your story or the stage of your illness, you deserve help. Research has shown that the sooner a person gets help the better their chance of recovery, so please don't wait to access that support or to reach out to those around you.

The UK's National Institute for Health and Care Excellence (NICE) has noted that early intervention leads to the best possible recovery outcome, with their guidelines stating: "Do not use single measures such as BMI or duration of illness to determine whether to offer treatment for an eating disorder."[5]

Every single person deserves help, regardless of their weight. And if support services are in place early, people are more likely to recover. Growing evidence suggests that eating disorders are associated with significant structural and functional brain changes. Eating disorder behaviours are initially rewarding, then habitual, and then neurocognitively engrained.

For more on how to access help, turn to Chapter 4.

#DumpTheScales

I started the #DumpTheScales movement after realizing that my story of being turned away from support services wasn't unique to me, but something that happens to hundreds of people every day across the world. Not only this, but I realized that people with eating disorders often feel misunderstood and misheard by those around them.

My #DumpTheScales movement (check out the hashtag on Instagram and Twitter) is about changing attitudes toward eating disorders and moving away from the weighing scales. Eating disorders are about control and numbing emotions, and it is important that no matter what size or shape someone is, they are able to get support if they need it.

---

5   NICE guideline NG69 (2017). Eating disorders: recognition and treatment. Available at: www.nice.org.uk/guidance/ng69/chapter/Recommendations

Through the work I do in hospitals, I meet individuals who have eating disorders (sometimes as the primary diagnosis, sometimes as the secondary) and so many of them talk openly about how hard it is to be taken seriously when their weight is going up, or if it didn't fall as low as someone else's. It is upsetting that we live in a society where people judge the severity of the mental state of an individual with an eating disorder by their weight. Jodie's story below is one of many that I hear daily. If this has happened to you, I hear you and I see you. I know how frustrating it is.

CASE STUDY: JODIE

Hiding behind various characterizations I had portrayed within my Performing Arts course was my safety net. Once I had finished the course in the summer of 2018, I no longer had that safety net and I felt exposed; the secret that I had hidden had surfaced and I felt like a lost little girl and it was at that time that I felt I needed help and I had to reach out. Weeks later, upon leaving my mental health assessment at my doctor 's surgery, my heart broke. I had been rejected because my BMI was too high for treatment. I felt judged and it made that voice in my head become louder and bully me more. This I could not bear; I had suffered from low self-esteem and body image from the age of 14. This was due to the trauma I had experienced and the impact of abnormalities my disability had upon my body. I had always been jealous of girls who could do things like cartwheels, handstands or even gymnastics to name a few of the activities I found challenging. This is one of the many reasons why I felt comfort within that eating disorder voice. It would convince me that I would be able to do all these things if I was a certain weight. After my rejection, I turned to the UK charity Beat, who kindly pointed me in the right direction of a local charity. Upon referral, I attended an assessment with a therapist and afterwards, half of me felt relief, but the other half still felt invalid. The therapist diagnosed me with atypical anorexia: due to the word "atypical", this still felt invalid as I did not meet the full criteria for 'proper' anorexia and I felt I was just not sick enough. My treatment with the organization consisted of individual and group therapy and I am still a service user three years on. They have helped me recognize that this is not my choice and that I do have a problem. I still find myself in a battle every day with the anorexic voice, but I know I have the strength to fight it.

For anyone who wants to reach out for help, my tips would be to:

- *Write things down that you want to get across during the assessment to help with nerves and, if possible, have a close relative or friend attend the assessment with you.*
- *Put anxieties aside – try listening to some inspirational music. For example, the song 'Brave' by Sara Bareilles helps me feel calm and relaxed.*
- *Speak up about how you are feeling to family and friends, as this will help you feel supported.*

Remember that eating disorders should never be based upon physical appearance and to be brave and keep fighting!

The solution to this issue is not simple or quick: we need to change guidance and understanding, and to improve early intervention. We need to ensure that eating disorders do not discriminate on the basis of weight and BMI. This will improve treatment and eating disorder rates of recovery and reduce mortality rates. It will encourage those who feel they might be discriminated against to reach out for support and will help to destigmatize how eating disorders are treated.

We all have a role to play in this across society to educate clinicians, policymakers, the public and the media on the realities of eating disorders being primarily a mental health issue – not just a weight issue.

EATING DISORDER MYTHS BUSTED

Eating disorders aren't just about weight

When I was 13 years old, I had body image issues but the main reason I first started skipping meals was to stop feeling things. I was fed up of family arguments and of not being completely happy with life. Skipping meals gave me reassurance and made me feel good again. These feelings were short-lived and looking back they didn't complete me at all, but at the time I certainly put all my energy into them.

Just because you can't see someone is struggling with food, doesn't mean they're not

I sit down at meals every day and the majority of the time I feel fine, but there are still some days when I struggle. Depending on someone's stage of recovery, these days will happen. I used to sit down to a meal, frantically add up the calories on the plate, fear flooding through me. I felt lost and alone and the guilt that followed was intense. But you get through it and you keep going. You have to talk about how the meals and general food make you feel.

Eating disorders are not a phase

Whatever anyone says, eating disorders are not just a phase people go through. They are a serious mental health problem and can be fatal.

Eating disorders can affect everyone

The perception of eating disorders is that they only affect teenage girls. The truth is that eating disorders can affect anyone of any age, any gender and any background.

You can't see yourself the way others do

I get up each day and look in the mirror. Some days I see a normal-sized, athletic-shaped girl. Other times I see a huge person staring back at me. Before I got admitted to hospital, I didn't think I was that thin. I didn't believe it when the outpatient teams told me I was going to die if I didn't start eating. When everyone said I looked so unwell I thought they were trying to make me fat. It was only after doing the drawing exercise (see pages 17–18), I realized that maybe my perception of myself was all wrong.

Eating disorders can dominate your entire life

They are about so much more than food. It is important that the problem is tackled head-on and that people are given time to recover.

Developing an eating disorder is not a choice

I didn't choose to have anorexia. No one chooses to have an eating disorder.

Sharing is hard but life is so much better when you do

Eating disorders are secretive and it can be hard to share with others. But find those people around you that you trust and confide in them. Bring them onside, let them in, and let them hold your hand when you feel like giving up.

There is so much more to recovery than just weight gain
The mental versus the physical side of eating disorders is hard work. So much of the battle goes on in your brain.

Recovery IS possible
When I was in hospital I never thought I would get out; I never thought I would have a day when I didn't feel fat or when I didn't let calorie counting dictate my entire life. But I have done it! Yes, I still have bad days and I have to manage my eating, but it has been worth it.

CAUSES OF EATING DISORDERS... FROM DR OBUAYA

- The common eating disorders, anorexia and bulimia nervosa, do run in certain families, so if you have a first-degree relative (parent or sibling) with the condition, you have a higher risk of developing it than the average person.
- The rate of sexual trauma is higher in people with anorexia nervosa and bulimia nervosa than in people not experiencing eating disorders.[6]
- There is not substantial evidence in the psychiatric literature that social media or traditional media platforms cause eating disorders.
- Historically, eating disorders were viewed as reflecting dysfunction within families. Within the psychiatric community it is now more common to think of family dynamics maintaining the eating disorder, but the genetic component being a much stronger causative factor.

---

6   Tice *et al* (1989). 'Sexual abuse in patients with eating disorders', *Psychiatry Med*, 7(4), pp. 257–267.

- Anorexia is ten times more common in women than men, for reasons that are not understood. However, the gap appears to be narrowing among younger people, with as many as 1 in 4 young people with anorexia being males, though it is difficult to estimate this accurately.

Wherever you are with your recovery, be patient, try and keep talking to those around you and give yourself time to recover. You may have reached a target weight or be out of the 'danger zone' according to medical professionals; you may have got your eating under control again and even be discharged from support services. All these things may be true, but the mental impact of an eating disorder always takes longer to catch up on than the physical weight gain or meal routines.

CHAPTER 3

WHERE ARE YOU NOW?

Most of you will have picked up this book because you have experienced an eating disorder. Perhaps you have had one yourself or you know someone who has. Perhaps you are starting out on the road to recovery, and have just left treatment. Or perhaps you were unable to get treatment so are fighting to recover on your own.

This chapter will encourage you to consider what stage you're at, what you have overcome, and to take stock of how much progress you have made. And be proud of it! There will still be things to overcome, but that's okay – these things take time! Recovery isn't a race.

While you read this chapter, I challenge you to try and remove some of that pressure you have put on yourself, and treat yourself with compassion and kindness.

TERMINOLOGY

Here's some terminology that you might hear people use in recovery. It might help you recognize what elements you still struggle with.

Recovery: For the purposes of this book, recovery is about being on a journey. It is about healing, and it is something that is attainable for everyone (no matter what our brains might tell us).

Functioning: Someone functioning in their recovery is at a plateau. They live their life still constrained by the rules and rituals of an eating disorder, but in such a way that they can live in society and out of treatment. A lot of people get stuck at this point because moving beyond it can feel scary. I plateaued for a very long time and had to actively push myself to move beyond this point.

Body-checking: This is the habit of constantly checking your body. Grabbing bits of it, measuring it, constantly looking at it in the mirror.

Compensatory behaviour: This is when we use an eating disorder behaviour, such as exercise, restriction or purging, to try to compensate for something we have done.

Fear foods: These are foods that we think will cause weight gain or impact our bodies significantly. Everyone has different fear foods, and different rules around them.

Healthy body weight: This is the body weight that is healthy for your body. I'm not basing this solely on BMI, but what is healthy for that individual as a whole. This includes things like your genetics and body type, and the weight which you feel mentally well at. It's different for everyone as there is not a calculator that can give you the answer!

However, we must be mindful that as individuals we need to make sure that we don't think a BMI of X is healthy for us if science goes against this.

Safe foods: Foods that an individual feels safe eating will be unique to them and tend not to trigger guilt or upset feelings.

Body image: How we think and feel in our bodies. It is our perception of ourselves and can often compare to the standards that we see in the world.

Where Are You Right Now in Your Recovery?

Many people judge recovery by appearance. You might be in the "healthy weight" bracket for your height, you might be eating meals without restricting, not bingeing or purging, but eating disorder recovery is about so much more than that. And even if you hit your "healthy weight", it might not be the weight for your body. We all have a different set point and we must remember as discussed earlier that BMI is extremely outdated. Your recovery from your eating disorder is best assessed by you, how you are doing mentally.

WHAT DOES IT FEEL LIKE TO BE IN RECOVERY?

I asked my Instagram followers what it meant to them to be in recovery, and I've included some of their answers below. Do any resonate with you? Notice that not all of the answers are positive, and lots of them are ongoing.

- Accepting myself for who I am
- Strength and empowerment
- Good sleep
- Having good days with bad days
- Discomfort
- Acceptance
- Freedom around food, and to do the things I really want to do without letting the eating disorder stop me

- A healthy relationship with food and exercise
- Not being scared of food
- Being kind to myself
- Doing the work
- Not using food as a form of control
- Doing things at my pace
- Forgiving myself
- Having a life worth living
- Rediscovering life without my eating disorder

For me, it is about freedom to eat what I want. It's about a life away from food. It's about getting up in the morning and not worrying about what I look like. It's about going out for last-minute meals and being able to exercise in a way that isn't punishing.

After I left hospital, I was a "functioning anorexic". I was regimented in my eating habits and exercise patterns. I ate in certain restaurants, had set meals in the week. While I was pretty happy with this set-up, I realized that there was so much more to life. I realized I wanted to really have complete food freedom.

What about you? Perhaps you are in this place too? Perhaps for so long you have felt afraid to listen to your body. It feels so hard at times to gain back that level of trust, but the more you push yourself the easier it will get.

EXERCISE 1: WHERE ARE YOU AT?

Take some time to think about the questions below and try and answer them. I'm going to ask you this question again at the end of the book, so keep it in mind.

1   What does recovery mean to you?

2   Where do you feel you are at?

3   Where do you want to be?

To help you answer these questions, ask yourself:
- How often do you think about food?
- Does food stop you going out?
- Do you limit social interactions because you are worried about food?

Do you think about exercise all the time?
How has your journey changed over the last few years?

- Think back to where your recovery started – how do things compare?

What are some positives and things you learned?

You might look at what you have written in the exercise above and it might make you feel uncomfortable. You might be disappointed that you still have a way to go until you feel you are "fully recovered" or you might think that what you want to achieve isn't ever possible. I certainly felt that. When I was in hospital, I remember a nurse asking me why I wanted to get well. I had some ideas in my head, but what stuck with me was that I questioned whether I would ever be happy? Would I ever be comfortable in my skin? Would I ever be able to live without calorie counting?

I want you to focus on your answer to question 1, and when we revisit this exercise at the end of the book, we'll see if your answers to questions 2 and 3 have shifted at all.

Try to use this book with the attitude of taking bold steps forward! Remember, you deserve to recover, and it *is* possible.

You Can Do This

I never thought recovery was achievable. Of course, I had seen people talking about being fully recovered, and how they were now relaxed around food, but I was always so sceptical. And to be honest there have been times along my journey when I have felt unsure. Those moments when something happens and you feel yourself slipping to that place again. For example, perhaps you feel yourself resorting back to your old eating habits after a particularly stressful time, but don't know how to stop yourself. This stuff takes time, but it's achievable and if I didn't believe it was possible, I wouldn't be writing this.

I used to stare in the mirrors in hospital and hate what I saw. I used to look longingly at my friends and be so jealous that they could just eat whatever with no care in the world. But do you know what? You can get to that point too. And you *can* get there and be happy. Yes, it takes time, and you might have some down days, but that's okay.

You can do this.

EXERCISE 2: A LETTER TO YOUR EATING DISORDER

I'm going to challenge you to write a letter to your eating disorder. Share all your feelings with it. Tell it how much you love it or hate it, what it has stopped you doing, where you feel it has helped you. Be real with yourself and honest.

This might feel uncomfortable and if it does, I suggest you write two letters: a positive one telling the eating disorder how much you "love" it, and then a negative one emphasizing how much you "hate" it. Here's mine:

Dear Eating Disorder,

I used to think you were my best friend. You gave me everything. You comforted me in the evenings when life felt so hard, you distracted me when my brain went to places I didn't want to go. For so long I thought you were keeping me alive... all those nights when you kept me going.

I don't know how I never realized what you were up to as our friendship progressed. As our relationship deepened. I was so sure you were the one thing in life that made everything okay...

... but no; you were the one thing in life slowly killing me. Slowly stopping me living. Emptying me out.

Your voice that had managed to seduce me, giving me false promises for so long...

Sometimes I long for it again. Sometimes I long to do what you wish. Sometimes I think back and wonder if you did really make me happy. But in those moments when you try and convince me of that, I won't let you!

I won't let you suck me back in! Not now, not ever. Even when you laugh at me as I look in the mirror, pulling out all the parts of myself I hate. Even when you convince me I am a failure, a waste of space... Even when you tell me that you can take away the pain... I won't let you come back!

Listening to you and living by your rules got me nowhere!

Anorexia, you are a manipulative bitch and whatever life throws at me, however rubbish you make me feel... you are not coming back!

Hope

Now, have a go yourself:

Getting Started

I know if you are anything like me you will want to start making changes immediately (and see the immediate results!), so before we move on to the next chapter, I want to share a few things that have helped me during recovery and that I think will help you:

Focus on the positives: I have tried this quite a few times, but in 2019 I made the effort to really do it properly. I found that by focusing on the positives, I felt more in control of turning around my mood. It wasn't always easy (and sometimes I had to blast Kelly Clarkson through my headphones), but it was about being proactive and pushing myself back into that positive mindset. It may feel impossible to begin with, but give it time because it does get easier. I carry a notebook in my bag so that I can write down positive statements and refer to them when I need to. I have a feel-good folder on my phone and a feel-good playlist on Spotify! There are also a few people I can text and say, "I don't feel so good" and also people that I can celebrate my wins with (including my most recent one, which was not crying when I spilt bin juice all over myself and the floor!).

Appreciate people: I used to spend so long beating myself up over the hurt I'd caused to loved ones. To stop the rumination, I learned to say sorry and then move forward. Quite often we blame ourselves for everything (sound familiar?) and it's important to let go of some of that and move on. Writing down what happened can also be cathartic.

Do something for yourself: I'd always tried to practise self-care, but eventually I made a conscious decision to actually do things for me! So, I stopped dropping my plans to swoop in to save others, and started doing things that made me happy. There is a fine line here, but it is essential to put yourself first and realize that it is not selfish to do so.

Challenge yourself daily: As I mentioned before, it is easy to plateau (see page 38) so once you feel this happening, begin to challenge yourself. I didn't just focus on food – I challenged myself about the clothes I wore, the restaurants I went to. I knew that I could do it if I put my mind to it and I was even more determined to crack this once and for all!

I may have made it sound so simple, but it isn't going to be. The realities of living in recovery are that there are highs *and* lows, but know that it is okay, and you can do it! I am finally cracking this once and for all and I feel so determined to not let my past dictate my future. I want you to feel like that too.

CHAPTER 4

ONGOING HELP

This book is not a replacement for professional support you may have had, are in the process of having, or still may be seeking, but it will help aid your recovery. It is important that we get to the root issue of how you feel in order to help you move into a space of true freedom. With all the types of support, feeling heard is so important. In this chapter, I am going to focus on professional support and therapy. You'll find information on other types of support on page 239.

Eating disorders are not always understood so being taken seriously and finding the right support can be difficult. Some doctors have told me to gain weight without any recognition that I may be struggling with an eating disorder, and with no understanding of the mental health issues behind it, which led me to be in quasi-recovery for a very long time before severely relapsing.

We often dismiss people because of their weight, but eating disorders are not only about weight. They aren't about being glamorous or about being a certain size. They are wrapped up in emotions and control, and this is why when we start to tackle them it takes time. Whatever your weight, size or shape, I really encourage you to go to your doctor if you are struggling with food.

Getting Help From Your Doctor

We know that there is a postcode lottery when it comes to doctor support, so the level provided will depend on where you live, and a lot of your interactions might be dependent on your doctor's training or support services available in your area.

Going to your doctor can be really challenging and perhaps some of you haven't had the best time at your appointments. This can happen at any time throughout your recovery journey, and I want to empower you to take ownership when you go to the doctor. It shouldn't always be our responsibility to speak up, but the way society is means sometimes we have to. For example, we need to speak up if we don't feel sure about getting weighed at an appointment and talk through your options. The doctor might be able to accept a recent weigh in at home, or in a recent therapy session instead of an additional weigh in. In my doctor's notes it states that I don't get weighed (although in extreme circumstances I probably would be okay with it) but if I am going to pick up antibiotics and they ask to weigh me, I politely remind them that I was weighed six months ago and so weighing me is necessary. Please be aware that it has taken a long time to get to this point, and to gain that trust from my doctor to not weigh me. I also just want to flag that in some cases a doctor will want to weigh you, particularly if you are in the early stages of recovery, and I do think it is important to trust them with this.

I don't know what your background is: whether you are at the start of your journey or you have been through treatment, are technically in recovery and want to go back to the doctor about your eating because it feels harder again. Whatever stage you are at, reaching out can feel difficult. It can be really challenging, especially as you might feel a real sense of guilt or failure around asking for help. I don't want to criticize support services, but I do want to share some of the things that have come up when people have reached out for support so that you know you are not alone!

Perhaps you've gone to a doctor's appointment, only to be told "You need to just stop all this now," or, "You really just need to eat." Or perhaps you've been told that "You need to put on X amount of weight." Do any of those statements sound familiar or make you squirm? I know they do for me! And it isn't anyone's fault – this isn't a blame game, but we both need to realize that the eating disorder has the potential to twist things that are said to us, *and also* call out when we are not being treated correctly by medical professionals.

I know that when I have been to the doctor in the past or even when someone has commented on my weight, my thoughts have spiralled. Eating disorders can make us look inward and we need to find a way to move our focus outward. To take a step back. If you go to the doctor and they say anything like the comments above, write it down, and then look at the evidence for why you need support.

Before you even get to your appointment, it is important to think about how to have that conversation. This is the same if you are relapsing, or you have been in treatment before and want the chance to be heard again.

It is *essential* that a plan is put in place when someone leaves support services or treatment, or when there is perhaps no referral in place. It is important to book another appointment with the doctor to ensure that you aren't left with a long period of time with no support.

FIVE TOP TIPS FOR DOCTOR'S APPOINTMENTS

1 **Write down what you want to say before you go.** That way you can read it out or hand it to the doctor without having to think quite as much. When I felt I was struggling again, I became quite matter of fact about it. Removing the emotion really helped me.

2 **Be clear.** Start sentences with:
- "My *mood* feels..."
- "I would like some *support*"
- "This has been happening for... *months/years*"
- "I feel like I am getting unwell again *because*..."

3 **Go with someone else.**
Taking someone with you may provide you with the courage you need to reach out for support. For example, they will be there to encourage you if you suddenly have a wobble and want to leave the waiting room. When your eating disorder makes you feel you shouldn't be asking for help or seeking support, they can provide another voice.

4 **Journal the experience.**
Spend some time writing about how it went and how you felt. This will help you process your feelings.

5 **Remember self-care.**
Do something for yourself afterwards and make sure you have a plan in place after the appointment to manage your own mental health.

Following your doctor's appointment, and depending on where you are with your eating disorder journey, you may be offered talking therapies (see below) or perhaps access support services as an outpatient or inpatient if your eating disorder is deemed actionable.

Remember to ask as many questions as you want to. Find out more about exactly what is being offered and what your options are.

What to Do if You Are Turned Away From Support Services

I've been there, and it's utterly crushing to get told you can't get any help. Here's my advice for if this happens to you:

1   **Be kind to yourself.** If you get turned away from support services remember that the eating disorder is going to blow everything out of proportion. It will guilt trip you, make you feel so awful and like a failure! But hang in there.
2   **Turn to your support network.** Don't try to deal with it all alone.
3   **Go back to the doctor.** You have a right to the treatment and deserve it. Write down your concerns, ask them to listen, and ask them to make a plan. For me this included going on medication, and going back to my doctor every few weeks. Being a bit forceful goes a long way. Again, I know how hard that might seem, so take someone with you for support if you can.
4   **Book an exciting trip or activity.** Something that will help you look forward to the future. When I relapsed in 2016 I remember meeting up with a friend for coffee. She asked me what was going on and I was honest. She then said, "We will get through this. Let's have a really fun summer and book loads in!" And it helped so much to create memories away from food.

Whatever the outcome of seeing your doctor, you need to work out how to keep communicating with those around you (see Chapter 5).

Therapy

If you are not in a place where you need outpatient or inpatient treatment, you may be offered some form of talking therapy on the NHS. This may be for a limited period only, and there will often be a long wait. You may want to seek out a private therapist in the meanwhile but, of course, that comes at a cost... The NHS also advise against seeing more than one therapist at a time, so you may experience that you find a private therapist, and see them until you get offered therapy on the NHS. You then need to make a choice whether to use your NHS place (and stop seeing your private therapist for those eight or so weeks) or carry on with your private therapist and bear the cost. By this time you've probably built up a relationship with your therapist and moving to another can seem pretty daunting. And there lies a big problem with the system!

It is so interesting speaking to people about their experiences of therapy. There are no two stories the same. Here's what some people have told me:

- "I felt really understood when talking with my counsellor as they were very empathic and reassuring that my mental health was not my fault."
- "Like a good pair of shoes, therapy took me quite a while to find the right fit but, once I did, I was taking lots of steps forward."
- "Therapy is exhausting, emotional and thought-provoking. It's not easy but it does work if you find the right person."
- "I've had two rounds, four years apart. It's been vastly helpful and helped me realize and solve the problems I was facing. It reassured me I wasn't in the wrong."

MY THERAPY JOURNEY

I have had a wide range of therapy. At nine years old I saw my first therapist (see page 9); at 17 I sat opposite another therapist, and remember telling him, "I am fine! Life is fine! Everything is just fine!" I used to hate those sessions, because I didn't *want* to talk. In hospital I experienced different kinds of therapy, from face-to-face talking therapy, to dance therapy, to some pretty awful family therapy, which turned into constant family arguments!

It's funny really, because if you knew me you would most likely think I am someone who loves therapy. Having spent a year in hospital recovering from anorexia and because I am a mental health campaigner, I must surely love therapy, right? While I have always believed some people need therapy, and therapy works for many, I didn't always put myself in that camp. Instead, I was someone who thought I knew what my coping mechanisms were and what I needed to do. I thought I had everything sorted; I knew what my triggers were, I knew the power of talking, and I also knew about moving forward in the right direction. Well that's what I thought… and how far wrong could I be!

In 2019 I began to really struggle, and saying yes to therapy felt so difficult for me back then. I was scared about talking, sharing my whole life, and opening up this complete can of worms from my past that I had never really dealt with. But I knew that if I didn't do it now, I was going to continue my life with a lot of unresolved issues. Therapy was about to be part of my next stage of healing. People often ask me why I didn't talk about being sexually abused as a child when I was in hospital, and I honestly find that hard to answer. We all have these parts of us that we don't want people to know about, the parts where there is just so much shame. It is those parts that maybe take a bit longer to come up, and a bit more time to process. I think it had a lot to do with age and maturing. You reach a point of realizing you have lost so much in life that you know you need to seek support and talk more.

I never thought I would say this, but I actually love my therapy this time round. I look forward to my sessions and having the space to talk openly about how I feel. I have let my guard completely down, more than I have ever done before, and it has helped to not focus solely on eating disorders. My therapy is person-centred and I choose to travel to Norwich for it. This was originally because I couldn't find someone in London, but actually making that effort to go has really helped me.

Before COVID-19 struck and all therapy moved online, I had my therapy routine down to a tee. I would get up at 6 am, get the tube to Liverpool Street Station, then a two-hour train to Norwich, get picked up by my therapist at the station, drive to her therapy room, spend a few hours there and then head back. It was pretty much a whole day out, but the routine allowed me to focus on myself for the day and have time either side to process things. When I had to do therapy remotely, I was petrified! But I managed and adapted.

I am not going to sit here and tell you it has been plain sailing because it hasn't, and some sessions are really difficult, but I also know that is all part of therapy.

THERAPY WHILE UNDER EATING DISORDER SERVICES

It will be especially hard for you if you are in support under an eating disorder service, or you are still having to weigh yourself and report back. The guilt around "reporting back" and being honest is very real, but try to focus on the end goal. Remember that it won't do you any favours to go back to the point of hiding your eating disorder. Brutal, aren't I? Keep talking to your team about it; be honest about how you are feeling about weighing yourself.

TYPES OF THERAPY

There are many different types of therapy for treating eating disorders. There is no consensus on what should be offered or, actually, what works. It's really important to find what works for you.

You might be limited to what you are offered through your local health service – and you'll find different areas favour different approaches! Some might offer you psychodynamic therapy, because that's what they've always done rather than being evidence-based!

Different types of therapy include individual, group and family therapy.

Within individual therapy there are different methods that you might be offered. These include:

- **Cognitive behavioural therapy** (CBT), where you'll learn techniques to help you work through negative thinking.
- **Psychodynamic therapy**, which explores unconscious processes that might be impacting on your eating disorder.
- **Person-centred therapy** (sometimes called counselling), focusing on active listening (making sure someone feels really heard), a non-judgemental, empathic approach, and helping someone to find their own way through their problems rather than providing solutions/advice.

You might also be shown how mindfulness can be used to help your mental health, encouraging you to pay attention to the present moment, and become aware of and sit with your feelings, without judgement.

As well as individual therapy, group therapy or peer support groups are commonly offered for those experiencing an eating disorder. This might include:

- **Family therapy**, which brings together the family to help solve family issues, and problems with communication.
- **Interpersonal therapy** – this is a structured therapy that takes between 12 and 16 weeks and focuses on the patient's relationship with family and friends.
- **Group therapy**, where you meet with several other patients to discuss problems and challenges, and reflect on how you have been feeling. Group therapy might also take on the form of a course or workshops where people have the chance to discuss their feelings and thoughts at the end.
- **Support groups** – this is more informal than group therapy and involves meeting to share advice and guidance. Please be mindful when you do support groups that you are in the right headspace so you don't end up competing with or feeling pressured from others.

See page 239 for more information on where to find a support group, and where to go to seek help.

I cannot reiterate enough the power of finding what works for you. For example, I always had reservations about group work because of the competitive aspect of eating disorders, but for others peer support has been really helpful.

Finding someone you trust and are able to build that rapport with and let your guard totally down is vital, so don't be afraid to change therapist if the relationship just isn't there for you. When I relapsed in 2016, I saw a therapist for a few weeks and we just didn't really connect, so I told her it wasn't working for me. It can feel hard to do that, but try to be bold because you do matter!

REMOTE THERAPY

At the time of writing, we are in lockdown from COVID-19. All therapy and counselling sessions have moved online, or to telephone sessions. I don't know when face-to-face therapy will begin again or if therapy will ever go back to what it used to be. Certainly, video therapy has been tried and tested by the masses, and most people haven't found it as bad as they thought they would! I actually think "normalizing" online therapy will help those who want to access therapy, but struggle to find time.

The reality for me was that I was terrified of doing my therapy remotely. I had no idea how it would work. How could I do it sitting in my room with my partner in the room next door? But it actually worked really well and I get so much out of it still. I choose to do mine over the phone, but ask for video counselling if that works better for you.

I want to share some tips on remote therapy:

1   Find an activity to do during the therapy if you struggle to concentrate or you get distracted by your phone. I always paint my nails during mine.

2   Make sure you have a safe space – it is important to view
    the therapy as the same as you would do if it was face to
    face. I live in a tiny flat in London so finding space was
    hard – I knew no one would listen in, but I didn't know if I
    could always be honest with someone else around. Most
    weeks I find a quiet corner in the gardens where I live,
    or one week I went for a walk. Do what works best for
    you. Find your spot or mix it up. I know some people find
    sitting in a car works just as well.

3   Treat it the same as a face-to-face session: for me this included
    having 30 minutes before and after to process my thoughts. I
    did this by walking or sitting down and journalling.

Overcoming Barriers to Therapy

Once I'd got over the stigma of having therapy, I began to make
other excuses. Do I really have the time? Do I have the money?
I am sure you have been there too, working it out, finding every
excuse under the sun not to go.

I felt guilty for spending money and taking time out for therapy
when I felt I should be working, but sometimes we need to move
away from the "should" and "should nots" and into a space where
we feel okay about taking time for ourselves and spending money
on our wellbeing. When I went back to therapy in June 2019, I
was terrified about opening up a can of worms. I was worried
about the cost, and I was afraid of it not working. I agreed to do a
month of intense therapy, but then ended up staying for another
year working through things. It was hard at times – therapy is –
but the more I processed things, the better it felt.

You might be reading this, thinking, well I have managed this far,
I don't think I need to get any deeper, but I promise you that you
will feel so much better if you can properly start to unload things.

You might also be thinking, "I'd love therapy but I can't afford it." I know that is hard sometimes and I also know that I am lucky that I can afford a therapist, but I had to make cutbacks elsewhere and for me it was about prioritizing. I stopped buying coffees and had my hair done less often. However, don't spend so much on therapy that it then causes you more stress in the long run financially. Remember that the cost of therapy varies massively by location and you may be able to access some free therapy, either on the NHS or through a charity (see page 239 for where to look).

If you've had therapy before that didn't work out, think about why and what you would like to be different. Talk to others about their experiences of therapy and perhaps try a different type or a new therapist.

TOP TIPS FOR THERAPY

- **Preparation time before and processing time after is key:** That was one of the best things about travelling all the way from London to Norwich for my therapy, as I had no choice but to reflect on the train on the way back.
- **Schedule in downtime after therapy:** This might be hard if you are working, or if you have a family, but try to schedule yourself at least 30 minutes afterwards for self-care.
- **Journal or find your own way to process inbetween sessions:** For me this normally involves lots of journalling and then going for a walk to give me thinking space.
- **Feel in a safe place:** If the therapy is remote, then find a spot to do it where you feel safe to speak openly without being overheard.

So many of us spend a lot of time thinking about therapy, about how helpful it would be. Maybe we comment on how others have it and we don't. You can have it too, so no more excuses! It might be a waiting game to access therapy, but there are various services out there and different types that are accessible (see page 239), so make it and yourself a priority.

CHAPTER 5

FRIENDS AND FAMILY

Having the support of friends and family in recovery is vital, but it can also be annoying and frustrating! You might feel that those around you are "keeping an eye on you" out of concern for your recovery. Or you might feel that no one is really helping at all, and become worried that everyone thinks that you are okay!

I certainly found it hard, because I didn't want loved ones to interfere, but I also wanted them to know that I wasn't totally okay. Getting the balance right is hard work, but once we cracked it, it felt good to have support.

Before we explore the role of family and friends further, I want to highlight a few do's and don'ts when it comes to eating disorder support. You may want to show this to those close to you. I do this so that others in my life will see those things that do and don't help me.

THINGS NOT TO SAY TO SOMEONE WITH AN EATING DISORDER

- You look much healthier than the last time I saw you. (This is completely triggering.)
- You are not eating/eating enough. (When said in a social situation this can be challenging as it draws attention to it in a group of people.)
- You are so skinny – just eat something!

- What's your secret to losing weight? I need it. (Followed by pointing out parts of their body they are unhappy with.)
- I was lovely and skinny like you when I was younger... (Especially from family members.)
- You are the same weight as you were when you were aged 13. (To an 18-year-old.)
- We will just put you on medication.
- You don't look thin.
- Eating disorders are chronic illnesses. (When people say this we lose all hope for recovery!)
- You don't look like you have an eating disorder. (It is important to not just focus on the body but remember that eating disorders are a mental illness.)

The Importance of Trust

When I left hospital, I decided to go straight to university. I took my A-levels in hospital as I wanted to feel like I was still moving forward in my life. I wanted to get back in sync with my friends and have a fresh start. This was probably a bit of added pressure that I had placed on myself, but my parents supported me. We had to start gaining each other's trust, and work out how to manage my anorexia. My parents had to trust me that at university I would keep eating and that I would be able to manage myself. They had to trust me and I had to let them in. We came up with a plan that I would text them weekly to tell them how I had been, then on really hard days I would send a simple message saying, "I am not okay". Despite knowing they couldn't fix what was going on, sending such a text would help me voice my feelings and be honest with them.

You may be living on your own, with your family or with friends. Whatever your situation, if you are coming out of treatment you need to learn to open up to at least a few people who you can trust and who trust you.

Take your time getting to know yourself again, and getting to know the people around you so that you can get the right support. For me this was even more important as I wasn't constantly being watched when I was discharged but was having to adapt to new situations and new relationships.

We need to let people in, but in such a way that it feels safe and genuine.

HIGH EE IN ANOREXIA... FROM DR OBUAYA

Expressed emotion (EE) is a concept established in the psychiatric literature to understand the impact of a relative's interaction with the patient. It is important to stress that this is not to blame families for the eating disorder, which is unhelpful, but a way of supporting families to move forward together.

It is defined as: critical comments, hostility, emotional overinvolvement, positive remarks and warmth.

In anorexia, "high EE", i.e. families making critical comments, expressing more hostility and displaying perceived emotional overinvolvement, is associated with poorer treatment outcomes.

Expressed emotion has been shown to impact treatment outcome for patients with a variety of psychiatric and physical illnesses. In families of patients with schizophrenia and depression, the level of EE has been found to be a robust predictor of relapse.[7] In families of patients with anorexia, high parental EE has been associated with treatment dropout and poor treatment outcome.[8]

---

7   Butzlaff RL, Hooley JM (1998). Expressed emotion and psychiatric relapse: a meta-analysis. *Archives of General Psychiatry*, 55(6), pp. 547–52.

8   Le Grange D *et al* (1992). Family criticism and self-starvation: A study of expressed emotion. *Journal of Family Therapy*, 14(2), pp. 177–192.

THE IMPACT OF LOW WEIGHT... FROM DR OBUAYA

The psychological consequences of remaining at a low weight for a prolonged period of time include: poor concentration; irritability; inflexibility; and social withdrawal.

The physical consequences of remaining at a low weight for a prolonged period of time include: a loss of bone strength, increasing the risk of osteoporosis and fractures; muscle wastage; hair loss on the scalp and hair growth on the face and arms; a low blood pressure and pulse; a lowered body temperature; and infertility. These effects are reversible as weight is restored.

We talk about romantic relationships later in this book but with friends it is always important to think about how much we feel okay sharing. There is a difference when sharing with someone because you are ready to and are prepared to be vulnerable, and creating some sort of co-dependency on that person. If you feel that things are moving too fast and you feel you are sharing too much too soon, speak up and say so!

Communication

Eating disorders thrive off isolation and have a way of twisting how we feel, so communicating with others in recovery is key. It takes time, but it does get easier. You need to work out what works for you and how much you want people to check in with you and inform you. For example, it is okay to ask your friends or family which restaurant you are going to, or what is for dinner. I sometimes felt silly asking, but by doing so I was able to have a better day and not be so stressed. I went from wanting to know exactly what time meals would be, what restaurants we were going to, to being able to be a bit more last-minute and spontaneous. But again, this is a process. It will take time and be different for everyone. It may help to have someone to help you with your food shopping and meal preparation each week. Needing such support does not make you weak – in fact, it will help you to feel more empowered and able to move forward.

Remember, there may be times when communication breaks down and things don't go to plan – those supporting you may sometimes get it wrong and that is okay. When you are supporting someone with an eating disorder, it can be hard. There have been times when I have gone home and meals haven't gone to plan and I have shouted (a lot). I have stormed upstairs to my room, stayed there, cried, and felt unloved. You might have experienced this too. It is hard and might feel frustrating when things don't go to plan, but remember it will be okay. Write down how you are feeling, offload on to someone, find support online if that's helpful, and the next day get up and start with a clean slate.

Dealing with a mental illness will be hard for everyone around you – your family, friends and colleagues. I am not saying this to make you feel bad, but it is the reality. People will try to fix you, they will try to have a conversation with you about it, and you might well be dismissive.

So how can we start to bring these conversations into the everyday to help normalize them?

Firstly, discuss your wellbeing with those around you; this is about prevention! You don't have to share your whole history, but find a way to bring these conversations into everyday life. I know that having space to talk about how I felt would have helped massively.

Secondly, make space to communicate without other distractions. I know that this might seem hard at times, but it is important. When I was first in treatment, we had to adapt my rather chaotic family life to find the space to talk. My mum and I would go for a walk and talk, and these conversations with her have become essential to my recovery. I still might try to be a bit shut off from others when it comes to sharing my emotions, but the more I have talked and opened up the easier it has been to keep going in my recovery. Another way of doing this is to send an email, which is something I do. It might simply say:

Hi,

I hope you are well.

I just wanted to share that I am struggling quite a bit mentally at the moment. I don't feel ready to talk about it yet as it feels easier right now to just plod on and keep going but I did want to tell someone.

I am hoping that from [INSERT DATE] I will start to feel okay again and, if not, I will reassess my [therapy, support or medication]. But just telling you so that you are aware.

Please don't worry about responding to this email.

Thank you.

Whenever I send these emails, I get a bit stressed and worried, but it always helps in the long run to share what is going on. I believe that the more we do this, the more it will help normalize the conversations around eating disorders.

Difficult Conversations

We live in a society where there is a lot of attention on calories and image; where people are constantly being judged. We need to be bold and push back when friends and family focus on dieting, exercise and calories… it is frustrating, but we must remember to distance ourselves. We cannot expect friends to get this right all the time, so we have to find a coping mechanism. Here are a few examples of things you could try:

- Try to change the subject – think of a go-to subject to bring up, like your favourite TV programme at the moment, to see if you can change the direction of the conversation.
- Say mantras to yourself when friends or family discuss food or diet. Try something like: "Everybody is different and needs different amounts of food" or "You don't want to let the eating disorder pull you back in" or "Winning at recovery is so much more important that letting one person cause you stress".
- Try to seat yourself with people who you know won't talk about dieting and food portions.

I WISH MY FAMILY KNEW...

I asked some of my Instagram followers what would be the one thing they would tell their friends or family about their eating disorder and here is what they said:

- It's not about weight.
- It is the scariest and loneliest thing ever.
- It is such a horrible existence.
- Eating disorders are not all about food and wanting to be pretty.
- You can have an eating disorder and not be underweight.
- Outward appearance doesn't count: just because we look okay or healthy, it doesn't mean we are.
- It is usually when I am at my healthiest that I am in a worse place mentally.
- However much we try, sometimes we have no control.

- An eating disorder is a mental illness and not something I chose.
- It's hard to give in to finally committing to get better.

If any of these resonate with you, think about including one or two in the above email to your loved one.

Having support in recovery from an eating disorder is really important but at times help can be hard to accept. You will have your own reasons for this – perhaps you have been hurt before or perhaps you think you are better doing this alone. I totally get this, and that is how I have been tempted to think in the past but over time this does lessen and the fear of speaking up also lessens. Throughout all of this, communication is key. Look at your support networks, work out who is around you and what roles people can play. How can individual people support you in such a way that it works for you?

Communication is hard, but the more we keep it open, the better it is.

CHAPTER 6

PARENTING PERSPECTIVE

This chapter is written for parents and carers. You may want to read it with the person that you are supporting or read it through and take some time afterwards to discuss what comes up, but please don't put pressure on yourself or them to do this. I probably wouldn't have done it with my family, but it might help you.

CASE STUDY: SUE

I knew that my 12-year-old daughter needed help a couple of months after she gave up chocolate for Lent and things escalated. We visited the doctor a couple of times but were told that her weight wasn't low enough to worry about and it was likely a phase. If only I had known what I now know, perhaps our heartache could have been avoided. Eating disorders are a serious mental illness, not a fad. I eventually got the help my daughter needed but it was a long, painful road. I learned that a calm, compassionate environment is vital and I learned skills to actively support my daughter to eat. Janet Treasure's stages of recovery helped me understand that part of my role was to encourage belief that recovery is possible. My daughter would show glimpses of being ready to change her eating disorder behaviours and then needed help to discuss how she could implement it. I

---

learned that cognitive function is poor at a low weight and that full recovery is difficult until weight is restored. Nothing can prepare you for your child battling an eating disorder. The despair, sadness and grief can be overwhelming but it is nothing compared to what the individual is suffering. There are some great trauma therapies that can support recovery. Compassion, kindness, patience and resilience are key. Standing alongside them for as long as it takes makes a real difference. Looking after yourself and asking for support is important too.

I can't imagine how difficult it is for parents and carers who are currently navigating caring for a loved one with an eating disorder and I am not going to pretend I know how that feels. I want to start by flagging a few things that are an important part of support:

- **Listen and don't jump to conclusions.** Be mindful that we don't want to be fixed; we often just want someone next to us, walking alongside us, offering support and listening. Please don't assume you know why something has triggered us.
- **Ask open-ended questions.** These give us space to feel heard and to talk it through with no constraints.
- **Check in with us.** We do not want to be constantly watched, but having check-ins will help us move further forward and help us feel heard.
- **Motivate us.** Help us think of reasons for wanting to get well and stay well. Sometimes we find these hard to think about.
- **Show us you understand.** Remind us that you know it is not about the weight.
- **Be committed.** Let us know that you will be there for us no matter what.

Feeling Helpless

It is so challenging watching a loved one struggling and realizing that they may not want to be fixed, that they will push you away constantly. When I was unwell, I used to behave so badly. I shouted a lot, blamed my family, threw food around... I would cook for hours, make the kitchen messy, and then leave it all. I was obsessed with feeding everyone else, but felt so afraid of the actual food.

I remember those weeks before I got admitted to hospital, where I would sit on the bathroom floor making myself sick, making sure that everything was out of my body. I knew that everyone was aware of what I was doing, but no one understood how to help. I didn't want help at this point. I used to blast the radio in the shower in the hope that people would not hear me, then emerge hours later with bloodshot eyes, tired and emotionally exhausted. If I couldn't get into the bathroom quickly enough, I would get so agitated with people around me. I hated what the eating disorder did to me, and how it made me react to people I really cared about, but the eating disorder always won.

There were moments when I would be standing and shouting at my parents as they tried to encourage me to eat. Shouting and shouting, throwing food around, watching their eyes fill with tears. There are evenings that really stand out for me, when I think the real me that was buried deep down tried to come back; the evenings when I would start to care about the fact my parents were crying. But when that emotion came up the anorexia would suck me back in. Holding me together. Helping me be "strong".

CASE STUDY: JOHN

For Alex, anorexia was part of a complex mental health picture. My son had developed anxiety in the last years of primary school, and we discovered he was cutting his arms and legs. CAMHs became involved and were helpful.

*But when he went to senior school in September 2017, we
started to spot unusual behaviours. His weight began to fall
too. We tried to talk to him, but we couldn't get anywhere.
At first, there was no progress. Alex began disappearing after
meals to vomit in the bathroom. When we realized, he found
other ways to empty his stomach, including out of windows.*

*It became a constant battle, but we kept in mind that it
was the illness making him do these things, it wasn't Alex
himself. The family began receiving at-home nursing support
from late 2018, as another option to hospital admission.
For Alex, the intense work began to pay off and he had a
"moment of clarity" and started to talk about taking back
control of his life from the illness.*

*He's made good progress – I'm pleased when he's cheeky
now. Sometimes he even asks for a beer on a Sunday
afternoon. We have our life back to some extent but we're not
complacent. Sometimes I have to pinch myself we've come
this far.*

*I would describe the anorexia experienced by Alex as a
"manifestation" – almost like a possession. Alex was totally
overtaken by the illness and we were all caught – him included
– in a battle against it. Thank goodness, every day, I see more
and more of him coming back.*

I am sure you can relate to these stories, the hardship, the pain
… and perhaps those feelings of isolation. It is so, so difficult
and one of the hardest questions to be asked because there is no
definitive answer is "How do I fix my child's eating disorder; how
do I make them accept they have a problem?"

I certainly do not have all the answers, but what I do know is
that with the right support and interventions in place, recovery
is possible.

During my work with parents through schools and hospitals, similar issues come up and I wanted to share these with you now, for two reasons: firstly, in the hope that you will feel less alone; and secondly, to try to provide some solutions.

ISSUES YOU MAY FACE

ISSUE	SOLUTION
Your child chooses one parent as a carer while the other person gets blamed (especially when the young person starts to play you off against each other)	Make sure you keep dialogue open and present yourselves as a team.
A sense of being judged as a parent	Judgement is so hard at times and you might be reading this feeling like you have failed your child or loved one. But you haven't. Find the support you need and remember that there are others going through this right now. Even though your story feels so hard, you aren't alone.
Poor communication with support services	Ask for a care plan. It is your right to know what the follow-up will be. If your child/loved one is aged over 18, discuss having access to their medical records, with the express consent of your loved one. I highly recommend doing this when they are just leaving treatment so that if things get harder, they won't be able to shut themselves off.
Impact on wider family	Create happy memories with the whole family. Do things that don't involve food so that everyone can be involved. Communication with other family members is so important. Bring everyone into what is going on and make sure you are giving time to other people at home.

ISSUE	SOLUTION
Wanting to fix the problem	Don't try to totally fix us – I know this goes against everything you might be feeling, but we don't always want to be fixed. We want to be listened to and held. When we are crying in our rooms over something we have eaten today, please don't go into practical mode, but just hold us while we cry. Patience is key!
Feeling isolated with a real lack of support	Find support online or in person – see page 239.

So, as a Parent, What Can You Do?

EDUCATE YOURSELF

We aren't asking you to know everything about our eating disorder, but trying to understand bits of it will help us feel like you are taking it seriously. Read books, research on the internet, read blogs, listen to podcasts; there is information out there. For us, the important thing is that you are trying to understand what it is like inside our brains; the fact that we have this constant battle going on in our heads; that sometimes we will act in a way which might hurt people around us, but we still care about them.

BUILD TRUST

This is key. We need to know that we can trust you to not make us change weight too fast and that you aren't feeding us more than we should have. We need to learn to trust that we can tell you anything and it is okay. And, above all, we need to know we can trust you that when we eat food you don't assume everything is 100% okay. Levels of trust will change over time and this will be something that everyone has to adapt to. If you are struggling with trusting the person you are supporting, start slowly by giving them some flexibility, let them go for dinner with their friends, or choose a snack they might want to have. When you do this make sure you still allow time to check in with them. Remind them that you know it might still be hard for them, but that you are there no matter what.

PLAN ACTIVITIES THAT DON'T INVOLVE FOOD

We live in a society where lots of events happen around food, which is extremely stressful for someone with an eating disorder. Support your loved one by varying things so that you can create positive, happy memories together without eating being part of the picture.

MEAL PLANS AND SET MEALTIMES

Let us plan meals with you and please don't change the menu or the times last minute. Eating disorders give us a real sense of control, and we may be facing huge anxiety around mealtimes – from the run-up to them to the feelings afterwards. Knowing when the meal is happening and what's on the menu helps to alleviate some of that fear.

When I first was in recovery, I was very regimented in this because it meant I knew what I would be eating throughout the day. This will change over time, but try to work with the person you are supporting. It is also worth remembering that certain times of the year may be harder for someone. For some reason I went through years of finding Christmas really hard. I could never pinpoint why, as I was always allowed to have my own meal or cook something I wanted. I am sure you have those times when you know the person you are supporting will find things harder and that's okay. It might also be quite unique to them. If this is the case, make sure you stick to the plans you have with food.

When I began recovery, I used to really struggle being at the dinner table for a long time. When a meal ended, I just wanted to get up and leave. I would often get really agitated if people were taking their time over the meal, particularly if I had found it challenging. Please be aware of this, and also aware that your loved one might not want to be alone after a mealtime. Distraction is key!

AVOID TALKING ABOUT PORTION SIZES, DIETS AND WEIGHT

This may seem completely harmless to you, but could have a hugely negative impact on our recovery!

DON'T IGNORE A NEED TO EXERCISE

If exercise is a problem for the person you are supporting, then speak to your local gym and clinical team about getting a couple of personal training sessions. I know this might seem risky and a bit ridiculous, but I found exercise hard to manage when I was unwell. I was obsessed with it for so long – I would work out endlessly and feel guilty if I didn't do enough. After ten months in hospital, I was allowed to do three short runs a week with Mandy, one of the nurses. It gave me the space to understand how to exercise in a healthy way, as well as giving me the space to talk about what to eat when I exercise. When I relapsed in 2016, I got myself a personal trainer to help get back on track. So often when someone has an eating disorder it helps them to have the evidence behind something. For me understanding exercise and then training in a healthy way began to help me further my recovery. See Chapter 15 for more on exercise.

HOLD OUR HAND THROUGH IT

Please don't give up on us! The fact is when you have an eating disorder you feel so unlovable a lot of the time. You are constantly pushing people away, and at times the shame gets too much so you push, push, push! When we do this please be patient with us. Give us space to feel and throughout this remind us you are there for us no matter what! Within this remind us that you love us. It sounds simple doesn't it, but so often we just need to hear those words!

HELP US TO COMMUNICATE OUR FEELINGS

We have spent so long showing our emotions through food, so we need to work together to find other ways. Something that might help is you beginning to share how *you* feel. Put aside some time every few days to check in; and put your entire focus on the person you are supporting. It will take time; these things always do, but I guarantee it will start to help.

LOOK AFTER YOURSELF

Within all of this it is so important that you look after yourself too. Find your support network; people who you trust and can be honest with too.

Looking after a young person with an eating disorder can be a complete and utter minefield, but it is possible. Despite the many tears and arguments, recovering from an eating disorder is worth fighting for.

What to Say to Your Loved One

"YOU ARE DOING REALLY WELL"

Hearing small words of encouragement is an acknowledgement that we are struggling. I know when I first started enjoying food at home, and relaxing at meal times, I was met with this guilt in my head. But we can challenge that guilt with your help by helping us feel that what we are doing isn't a bad thing. And that we don't have to show others we are not okay by not eating.

"I AM HERE IF YOU NEED ME"

This statement goes a long way to helping us not feel like a burden to others. I know I sometimes feel so bad when I struggle at what should be a nice, relaxing mealtime for everyone. It is when I feel bad about it that I stop talking.

"DO YOU WANT SOME HELP WITH PORTION SIZE?"

Portion size is a minefield! And nine years into my recovery there are still some portions I struggle with (I only eat individual-portion-sized yogurts and porridge). When you are in recovery, you don't want to eat too little or too much, so this question allows us the chance to accept we might need some help.

"LET'S DO AN ACTIVITY"

Distraction is always welcome – whether it is playing a board game, going for a walk or watching something on the TV together can always help. It may just help them snap out of what's going on in their head.

"WHAT CAN I DO TO HELP?"

Sometimes it feels like whatever you say or do won't help, so just being asked what exactly you need is a good thing.

PART 2
UNDERSTANDING YOURSELF

CHAPTER 7

IDENTIFYING YOUR TRIGGERS

What is it that makes you feel emotionally charged around food?
Is it the things people say or do, or certain events, that cause you
to binge-eat or restrict what you eat?

Being triggered is when an event or experience causes an
emotional response that is related to something from the past; it brings
back feelings from that time and may cause us to repeat behaviours.

Your eating disorder may be triggered by various things – for
me it tended to be eating out in restaurants or seeing people
working out online. You may not always know *why* you have
responded to something in a certain way, but once you become
aware of and accepting of your triggers, you will be more able to
handle your response to them – and this is a really important part
of recovery.

In this chapter, I'm going to look at some of the common
triggers around eating disorders, but be aware that triggers
are very individual and can change over time – mine
certainly have.

Conversations Around Dieting

Regardless of whether you have an eating disorder or not,
conversations around dieting and exercise can feel relentless at
times, and living in a society that constantly tells us to "shrink"
ourselves and that "skinny is best" can make it even more
difficult to get better from an eating disorder.

Conversations around diet and exercise and body image are bound to be triggering and they can be much more prevalent at particular times of the year – for example, the pressure to look good in a bikini in the summer or to fully embrace food festivities over Christmas. It can help to be even more prepared to be triggered at these times.

Stay mindful of who you surround yourself with, especially when you are feeling particularly vulnerable. We all have friends who talk about dieting too much and it's okay to step away from those people when you are struggling. If you can't physically get away, it's useful to know how to subtly change the subject. The next time someone starts talking about dieting and how much exercise they are doing, how about changing the topic?

CHANGE THE SUBJECT!

Here are some examples of what I normally change the subject to when dieting becomes the topic of conversation:

- Films and TV shows
- Catching up on family life
- The weather (because that is even more interesting than diet chat!)
- Think random: try a "Would you rather...?"

Add any others you can think of...

TRIGGERING COMMENTS

A triggering comment might be something like, "You look healthy!" or "You look well," or you may become triggered when someone comments on your weight. This can be a trigger because we equate the word healthy with looking like you are fine, or like everything is fixed, or that we now look too big to have had an eating disorder. Our brains blow these words up in our own minds and make it really difficult to keep going that day. While to them it might seem completely harmless, it might send your mind into overdrive as the eating disorder twists the words. For me now I am able to push through when people say these things but this has taken time and took a lot of self-reassurance at the beginning. I know how frustrating it might feel for you that so often people feel they can comment on appearance, particularly when eating disorders are about so much more than that.

Hearing someone declare "I earned that food" can also be triggering. When did food ever need to be earned? This unhelpful comment is often made at social gatherings and can be hard to avoid. When I worked in an office, I knew that during birthday celebrations the conversation would become focused on how people had earned the right to eat the cake. It used to annoy me because food isn't there to be earned – it's there to be enjoyed!

Triggering comments from family members are an example of high expressed emotion (see page 63).

NUMBERS – CALORIES, WEIGHTS... YOU NAME IT

Comments about the calorific content or size of food portions can be hugely triggering. For example, someone might say something seemingly "harmless" about the size of a pizza or sandwich. Your mind goes into turmoil. You stare down at the plate of food. You then start to try to justify it to yourself, telling yourself that tomorrow you can make up for it!

Or people might justify having an extra slice of cake by saying they will burn it off later, or they didn't have breakfast. Most people wouldn't bat an eyelid, but for someone with an eating disorder this can be hugely triggering. My family know not to talk like this around me, but other people don't always remember. I was with a friend recently who kept talking about how little she'd had to eat. No matter how far through my recovery I am, I still find this "weighing up" of food can derail me.

Other Common Triggers

Perhaps you can identify with some or all of the following. Later in the chapter, there is an exercise to help you work out your own triggers and your responses to them.

BEFORE AND AFTER PHOTOS
Do these make you feel pretty lousy? Whenever I see them, the competitive part of my brain kicks in making me feel useless, a bad anorexic, failing… I am sure you can complete the sentence.

EXERCISE
Exercising is a good thing and, as a society, we are encouraged to stay fit, but it can be triggering when people share every detail of their workouts on social media. When I see such posts, the competitive part of my brain kicks in, that part that tells me I am letting myself go if I'm not exercising, or that something will go wrong. As with all triggers, we can't change or remove them, but we can choose how we respond. At the beginning of my recovery, I would remind myself that others needed to exercise and keep in perspective the amount they were doing. I became aware that, whatever my brain was telling me, I didn't need to measure myself against people. It can help to rationalize in this way – perhaps write statements on the notes section of your phone that you can read when you feel challenged.

FEELING TRAPPED AND HAVING NO CONTROL
When you feel powerless, it is uncomfortable and the eating disorder will do its best to try to pull you back in. It tells you that it can give you the control you need, that it can help make

everything feel okay. Unfortunately, uncertainty and feelings of control are part of life. As I write this, we are still in lockdown because of COVID-19, a situation over which we have no control. At times like these, you will have to sit with triggering feelings, and it will take all of your strength to not get drawn into unhealthy coping mechanisms. When I had these feelings in the pandemic, I was absolutely terrified. Anorexia did what it could at the start to try and lull me back into that sense of security. But it failed because I talked, I brought it out into the open, and instead of feeling shame around my anorexia, I talked about it in such a way that *it* felt shame. And it slowly slunk back to where it belonged. When you are triggered by feeling out of control, there are things you can do, from going back to some sort of routine, to reaching out for support, to reminding yourself how far you have come.

PLANS CHANGING LAST MINUTE

In recovery, you may become quite set in certain routines and ways of dealing with food. I know I certainly did. When plans around mealtimes change, it can make us feel unheard and unloved; people act as if we are totally okay with things and this can be a trigger. A few years ago, I was at a family gathering and the plans changed last minute. I was confused and really upset by the whole event and I let my emotions get the better of me. Within these situations we need to remember not to take it personally. Bring your awareness to how you are being triggered and stick to your original meal plan as best as you can.

SPECIAL EVENTS

Certain events, such as family gatherings, and particular times of the year, such as Christmas, can trigger a whole heap of anxiety about food – from what will actually be served and at what time, to all the conversations around food. Planning is key – try to be involved and make your needs known. I also found it helped to have a self-care plan for afterwards, including someone I could turn to for support.

WEIGHING SCALES

For some reason we put so much emphasis and give over so much power to the weighing scales and they can be a huge trigger. First there is weighing ourselves or being weighed in treatment and recovery, and the feelings triggered by that. Second, there is that constant feeling that we *have* to weigh ourselves, despite the fact it will most likely make us feel really awful. We get stuck in this cycle of doing it and then when we don't do it we feel out of control.

SOCIAL MEDIA

When you are on social media, how do you feel? Do you follow accounts that make you feel worse? Is your feed full of people that you are comparing yourself to? When you have a bad day, do you mindlessly scroll? That was me for a very long time (and still is at times) but what I have realized is the more mindful I am of social media, the better it is for my wellbeing and the happier I am!

RELATIONSHIP ISSUES

Going through a break-up or having day-to-day relationship difficulties might trigger you to blame yourself and turn toward your eating disorder. You may feel unlovable and that the person will only see how much they have hurt you if you hurt yourself. I used to ruminate constantly, get my brain in a muddle, and beat myself up over what was happening, but that didn't help me or those around me. I didn't know how to express my feelings in the right way. I feared people would leave me and hurt me and it felt like the anorexia was the only thing that I had – I knew it would be there 24/7. It was only later that I discovered it held no value and was a very one-sided relationship. When you are feeling triggered in this way, it's important to love and value yourself and remember that you matter.

ARGUMENTS
An argument might trigger you to numb your feelings with food or exercise, only to find you are left feeling worse afterwards.

BODY COMPARISONS
Being on the beach or in a changing room, or seeing photos on social media or in magazines, is hard! Agreed? It leads to constantly body-checking and making comparisons, and yes of course we always come off worse!

STRESSFUL TIMES
We may feel triggered in stressful situations when we feel we have to strive to do our best, such as when taking exams, and if we feel we have little control over the outcome. I took my A-levels in hospital and, while it was challenging, it meant I was lucky to have amazing support around me. Even so, it felt so hard at times. Being aware of and prepared for how you are triggered during stressful times can help.

NOT FEELING HEARD
I spent a lot of my life not feeling heard and, as a result, ended up showing that I wasn't okay through not eating. Sometimes it feels like resorting to eating disorder behaviours is the best thing to do when people aren't listening to us, but I learned the hard way that good communication is key.

EXERCISE 3: IDENTIFYING TRIGGERS

In this exercise, I'd like you to identify the things that trigger you and reflect on how you respond to them.

1   **Identify:** Work out what triggered you. Even if it feels really small, make a note of it.
2   **Reflect:** Reflect on how you responded to the trigger. Is it something or someone that can be avoided? Or is it something or someone you need to face and find a different response?

Complete the table below. I've put one of my own examples at the top.

TRIGGER	FEELINGS	HOW HAVE I RESPONDED IN THE PAST?
e.g. Argument with someone I care about	Sad, frustrated, unheard and trapped	Restrict food and over-exercise so that people know I am not okay

TRIGGER	FEELINGS	HOW HAVE I RESPONDED IN THE PAST?

Dealing With Triggers

To reduce the chance of being triggered, try the following:

- Limit time with people whose conversations and comments tend to trigger you or, if it's an option, cut them out of your life altogether.
- Have a plan in place for the times of year you find difficult, perhaps when there is more focus on food or body image.
- Say no when you have to. Be aware that you might feel guilty about this, so make sure you have someone you can check in with. Focus on your self-care, and find a way to sit with the negative feelings and wait for them to pass.

BREAK THE BEHAVIOUR

Avoiding the things that trigger you will be helpful but, ideally, you need to break the connection between the trigger and the unhealthy behaviour – e.g. bingeing, purging, over-exercising

– altogether. This might have become your natural response to stressful situations and upsetting comments, and it might even seem okay and normal to you, but you need to ask yourself whether you want to keep responding in this way or whether you could choose to do something differently. If you are anything like me, when you respond in an unhealthy way to a trigger, you may end up feeling pretty guilty about it afterwards.

One way to break the behaviour is to replace it with another one. Here are some of the things that work for me:

- Journalling
- Going for a walk
- Going to a café
- Remembering that I have a plan – I am in control of my behaviour
- Reminding myself that there is no "right" way to feel
- Being kind to myself
- Turning to someone I trust

REWARD YOUR HARD WORK

Once the urge to respond to a trigger in an unhealthy way has passed, try to do something for yourself. Maybe have a soothing bath, or allow yourself to relax in front of the TV. Whatever it is, congratulate yourself on making it through.

There will be times when you feel triggered and go back to that unhealthy behaviour. If that happens, draw a line under it and try again the next day. It is important to show yourself self-compassion and not berate yourself.

EXERCISE 4: CHANGING YOUR BEHAVIOURAL RESPONSE

Take one of your triggers from the above exercise and think about how you could respond differently. Here's one of my examples:

Trigger: Hearing people talk about dieting and calorie-counting.

Unhealthy response: Restrict food or punish myself with exercise.

Healthy response: Journal how I'm feeling and confide in someone I trust.

Try the new behaviour and then reflect on how it made you feel? Did it feel hard or easy? If it was too difficult or not effective, come up with an alternative. Or have you written it, knowing that you probably won't respond in this way. What's stopping you?

The next time you feel triggered, revisit this exercise. Take a step back and process. Count to ten slowly, then rethink your response. The more you practise this, the easier it will get.

THINK B.L.A.S.T... FROM DR OBUAYA

Binges may be triggered by emotions. A useful tool to remember this is BLAST – you may want to ask if you are:

- **B**ored
- **L**onely
- **A**ngry
- **S**tressed, or
- **T**ired

It can be helpful to write a list of distraction techniques for each scenario, which will help you to avoid bingeing.

Remember...

Triggers are something that all of us face on a day to day and just because we have them doesn't make us weak. But within this remember that eating disorders also amplify these negative feelings and may make things feel harder at times.

Have your distractions in place when you feel triggered by things.

Make a note of the ways you have responded to triggers so you can see how far you have come!

CHAPTER 8

BREAKING THE HABIT OF COUNTING

When you have an eating disorder, numbers begin to pretty much rule your life and the constant calorie-counting, step-counting, and weighing yourself become hard habits to break.

The longer you live with an eating disorder and the more you repeat these habits and feel rewarded, the more engrained they become in your brain. Over time you don't need the rewards, but the habits remain something that you feel you have to do – an essential part of everyday life. Think about other day-to-day habits, such as brushing your teeth twice a day. As a child, someone had to encourage you to do this, remind you, perhaps reward you. And then eventually brushing your teeth became second nature. The good news is that habits are a learned behaviour so they can be unlearned.

Calorie-counting gradually became less of a habit when I went travelling and lived in Thailand for a year. I lived in a tiny village, volunteering for a children's centre, and there was just no chance whatsoever of counting any amount of calories! At first it felt really hard, but I slowly adapted to it and it massively helped my recovery, as I pushed those boundaries further each day. I realize not everyone has the luxury of travelling and living abroad, but it is about finding the best way for you of breaking the habit and moving forward.

Breaking the habit of counting is an important part of recovery and in this chapter I want to explore some practical, perhaps scary, things that you can do. Remember that recovery isn't easy and it isn't always linear, and you need to make changes at the right pace for you.

An Obsession With Numbers

Counting and measuring all aspects of our food and weight is a hard habit to break and even once you've stopped doing it to some degree, feeling slightly stressed or overwhelmed may trigger you to start again. I used to look down at my plate and work out the number of calories on my plate, before going on to work out exactly what every other person was eating!

We put so much emphasis on the numbers to give us contentment, but at the same time it makes us feel awful. It is sad and frustrating and so inward-looking. I found that when I went to an event where food was involved, I only remembered what I had eaten.

Counting can also numb emotions. I used it as a lifesaver when things felt really hard at home and, while I don't advocate doing it, I recognize that it serves a purpose. Once I didn't have the protective barrier of my counting habit, I had to learn to sit with and process what were often scary feelings.

WHAT WE THINK COUNTING GIVES US

I asked some of you what counting gave you and here is what you said:

- "It became a way of life, gave my day a clear structure, targets and parameters. It stopped me thinking and removed any element of spontaneous decision-making or uncertainty.* It removed choice, originality and freedom." (*Spoiler – it didn't work!)
- "It gave me a feeling of achievement and superiority."
- "As long as I had a target to reach, it gave me security."
- "It made me feel safe."
- "It made me feel worth something."
- "It helps me feel loved."
- "It helps me feel in control."
- "It numbed my emotions."

WHAT COUNTING ACTUALLY GIVES US

Now here's what some people said counting *actually* gave them:

- "It made me feel hopeless and trapped."
- "It made me feel isolated."
- "It made me feel bored."
- "It made my life extremely boring, restricted and repetitive."
- "It drained me of all energy."
- "I became distant at mealtimes."
- "It stressed me out and made me feel tired."
- "It numbed the good emotions as well as the bad ones."

EXERCISE 5: WHAT DOES COUNTING GIVE YOU?

Below you will see two circles: in the first one I would like you to write what you *think* counting does for you and in the second what it *actually* does.

Mine would look a bit like this:

Control
Value
Certainty
Reassurance
Love

Life limits
Taking up so much
of my headspace
Unhappiness
Stops me thinking about
other things

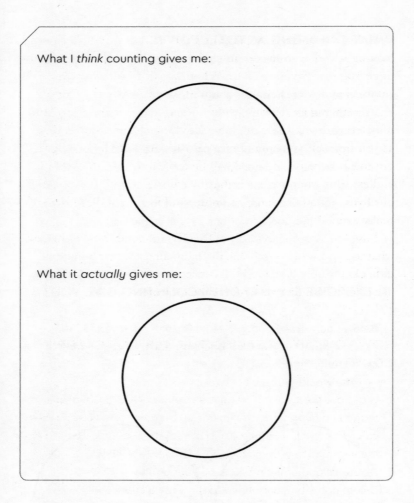

What I *think* counting gives me:

What it *actually* gives me:

Calorie-Counting

First let's look at the science. A calorie is a unit of measurement used to identify how much energy is in food or drinks. Everybody has a different body and therefore different calorific requirements. Realizing that everyone is different really helped me, especially when I compared the food on my plate to someone else's. The other thing to remember is that nutrition labels allow for a 20% margin of error!

Calorie-counting is something that the fitness industry push, making it feel even harder to change your behaviour or perhaps understand why you need to. When we start obsessing over calories, and we restrict the amount we can have in a day, we end up having an extremely closed and negative mindset. You may tell yourself you can't have anything else to eat that day as you have hit your maximum calories, or that you can't go out to eat because the meal will be too calorific... the list is endless. But what is clear is that by calorie-counting we restrict our lives, get a false sense of value, and lose sight of who we really are.

I used to look on enviously at friends and family who just knew what to eat. I wanted to break the habit after I left hospital, but didn't know how. The food still carried so much power and I felt like calorie-counting gave me so much control.

HOW TO START BREAKING THE HABIT OF CALORIE-COUNTING

1 Cross out the calorific information on packets of food in your fridge and cupboards. You might be thinking, "Well I know the calorie content without looking at the label," but by crossing out the information you will be a little less likely to check!
2 Delete calorie-counting apps on your phone.
3 Delete notes on your phone or throw away notebooks with records of your calorie-counting.

LEARN TO TRUST YOURSELF

Once you have done this, move on to the next stage. This is about listening to your body more and learning to trust yourself again. I would say this is one of the hardest things to do when recovering from an eating disorder.

Go outside of your comfort zone: Choose different foods whose calorific content you don't know. For me, this was so uncomfortable and stressful at first, but it helped.

Find distractions: Have a way of distracting yourself when you find yourself slipping back into the habit of calorie-counting. I would say something out loud to block my train of thought, or ask someone to tell me if I seemed disengaged at a mealtime. There have been points in my recovery when I have had to be really bold in speaking up and making myself stop doing this, and remind myself that the more I calorie-count the unhappier I actually am. If you find yourself calorie-counting outside of mealtimes, such as when you are lying in bed thinking about things, find strategies to deal with your thought patterns. I often find that the rumination starts when I feel overwhelmed with other parts of life and I get that false sense of control by calorie-counting. I make a list of everything on my mind (and that might include the meal I had three weeks ago). Writing it down doesn't necessarily solve it all, but it enables you to work out what exactly you are worried about and what you can and cannot control.

Be aware of triggers: Numbers and counting also links back to our triggers (see Chapter 7) – when life feels really difficult, you may want to start calorie-counting again to gain some control. At these points instead of writing down the amount of calories you are eating, write down your feelings. How does eating certain foods make you feel? And if they make you feel guilty, why is that?

Plan your meals in advance: This seems regimented, but it helped me move away from the daily fixation of calorie-counting and allowed me to move into a new place with food. I was able to start exploring what meals looked like across my whole week and I realized that eating a bit more one day and a bit less another didn't actually impact my weight, or the world around me.

Ignore others who may be calorie-counting: It is frustrating when those around you calorie-count, but you have to find a way to push through it. I often get out my phone and send a quick text venting about it or I might say something boldly, but overall try to find ways to not let it affect you, otherwise it is just another way your life is being dictated by calories.

Focus on the memories, not the calories: Don't make the memory of what you're eating all about the calories – focus on other aspects of the meal; the people you're with, the conversations, setting, etc.

DEALING WITH SHAME

There is a lot of shame around eating disorders – you may feel shame because you are calorie-counting even though you are a healthy weight or maybe you feel shame because you are so frustrated at yourself for still counting. We need to move away from a place of self-judgement to a place of self-compassion. From this point, we can start to explore how we feel around food and start to be curious about what foods might be out there, regardless of the calories.

Step-Counting

There are often so many feelings wrapped up in step-counting and Fitbit usage. This isn't necessarily an unhealthy habit for everyone, but for some it is one that soon gets out of control. We begin to obsess about how many steps we have done and start to feel bad about ourselves if we haven't done enough. We need to crack this before it gets to that point, because what the eating disorder tells us is normal, might actually be a dangerous ritual. When I stopped moving as much just to gain steps, I found I was less tired, and enjoyed walking more.

TIPS TO BREAK THE STEP-COUNTING HABIT:

1 Delete the step-counting apps on your phone or stop wearing your step-counting device.

2 Work out where you got the idea you had to walk a specific number of steps per day.

3 Challenge yourself to not leave your house at all; this will feel uncomfortable, but it is important to sit with those feelings and realize that the whole world isn't going to end and that your weight won't change just because you are not moving.

4 Use distraction techniques: when those feelings set in, distract yourself whether through writing, watching TV or playing a board game – whatever works for you.

5 Tell someone about it. The eating disorder wants you to keep it secret so that it can make you feel worse about it. So bring it into the light; make sure others know what is going on.

Weighing Yourself

Weighing ourselves seldom feels good, regardless of whether you have had an eating disorder or not. But for some reason we allow ourselves to be dictated to by those scales. We give them so much power, when actually they are doing more harm than good. Firstly, I want to emphasize that the weight on the scales isn't an accurate measure of our health. We live in a society that glorifies thinness, but actually scales don't tell the whole story; and don't even get me started on BMI!

So in recovery we need to move away from the scales, but with the acceptance and awareness that this might be a behaviour that comes back when life is stressful or overwhelming.

1 Bin your scales: perhaps make this into some kind of celebration event too! If binning your scales feels too hard, then begin to reduce the amount of times that you weigh yourself. Accept that your weight may fluctuate and that is normal but also remind yourself that there is so much more to life than this!

2 Tell someone: I find it helps to have people I am accountable to. Yes, it is annoying at times when they check in on your behaviour, but it also allows you to move forward in a healthier way.

3   Remind yourself that you are worth more than a number.
4   Spend some time working out why the number on the scales holds so much value.
5   Curate your social media feed so you aren't looking at the same sized people all day, and delete any of those accounts that trigger you to start making comparisons.

EXERCISE 6: REASONS TO STOP COUNTING

Make a list of all the benefits of not counting. I have made a start for you (please be as creative as you like!).

- You can enjoy your food more! Instead of looking at your plate as numbers, or risking your whole day being ruined because of weighing yourself, you can start to reduce the power counting and measuring have over you.
- It gives you more headspace to think about other things.
- It's not scientifically accurate to calorie-count.

Now add yours! This might feel uncomfortable, but dig deep and you will get there.

Remember...

1   Be intentional about breaking a counting habit.
2   Delete all counting apps and history on your phone, and throw away notebooks with data.
3   Do it your way. For example, I found it worked to have a day off from calorie-counting, and then a day on. Others like to stop

altogether in one go, and others like to tackle it meal by meal. Work out what works best for you, but remember longevity is key here!

4   Begin changing up your portions. For example, you might know that X pasta contains X calories. Instead of weighing it out exactly, try portioning out everything so you can estimate things, but in a way that makes the calorie-counting harder.

5   Have distractions in place when you feel like your mind may wander to calories again. This could be having friends joining you for dinner or knowing what times in the day you feel more vulnerable and staying busy.

6   Sit with difficult feelings and remember that you can do this!

7   Keep trying.

8   Keep challenging yourself when old habits or new food rituals try to creep in.

9   Be patient and kind to yourself throughout – these things take time to break and that is okay!

DEVELOPING HEALTHY HABITS... FROM DR OBUAYA

In developing and sustaining healthy habits (related to any key goal, not just nutrition), try to make the activity:

- Obvious – write it down and be specific (time and location); link it with an existing and established habit
- Attractive – pair it with something you really want to do; be around people that support the habit
- Easy – if the activity is quick, you are more likely to achieve it
- Satisfying – give yourself a reward for completing it (adapted from Atomic Habits by James Clear)[9]

9   **Clear, J (2018).** *Atomic Habits.* New York: Random House.

CHAPTER 9

BODY CHANGES

Eating disorders aren't caused by a negative body image – they aren't about being a certain size or losing weight, but the science and facts show that body image does become part of the illness, which is why I have included this chapter.

Many people, whether they have an eating disorder or not, put pressure on themselves to improve their body shape and compare themselves to others. I am no longer restricting my food, punishing my body or resorting to those old ways, but I do still have to navigate my body image. The aim of this chapter isn't to make you love your body, but I hope that it will help you to accept it and give you coping strategies for those challenging days.

CASE STUDY: BETH

Cheap, shiny, pink and white plastic chairs neatly lined the perimeter of the room and the windows were marked with water droplets and condensation. An inconsistent draft knocked the heavy wooden studio door partially open and shut, periodically allowing me to watch the older ballerinas inside the studio. It's these early memories that solidified my passion for performing. I knew from a young age that I didn't have a stereotypical dancer's physique. I was muscular, very busty, short, and had limited natural turnout. I had many dance friends growing up, but there was one in particular that caused me a lot of pain and overstayed their welcome. By nature, they were extremely competitive, I guess that's why befriending them was almost easy. They preyed upon my high-achieving qualities and used them to their advantage. Their companionship was enticing, with the promise of success in return for unwavering trust. It was clear to me that we shared a common goal – success.

This "friend" was anything but, and before I could fully process this, my long, arduous battle with an eating disorder had begun. What started as a love, quickly spiralled into a toxic relationship between my body, food and exercise. The mirrors we use for self-correction became a way for me to analyse every part of my being; my eating disorder fed me nothing but lies. I was constantly striving for perfection, but was taught that perfection is not a destination, therefore I would never be enough. The harder I'd work, the more pressure my eating disorder piled on. I believed that the skinnier I was, the better I'd dance, the higher my grades would be, the more opportunities I'd receive, but in truth, there is no correlation between my numerical value and my talent.

The full extent of my eating disorder went unnoticed for many years because I wasn't underweight. My relentless approach to exercise and "clean" eating was even applauded by friends and teachers. This encouragement only rallied my eating disorder on.

I'm learning to accept my body for what it is. Realizing that I'm not a talented dancer despite all these attributes, but that I'm a talented dancer in spite of them. So today when I step on stage or into the studio, I thank my legs that people once called bulky for allowing me to dance and I embrace my cellulite because it is natural, and my body fat doesn't determine my worth. My inability to fit into the stereotypical norms of the all-consuming, calorie-counting, toxic, body-shaming, dance world, this is what makes me a success, and this is something my eating disorder will never be able to take away from me again.

Not a Relapse

I had always been quite body conscious; I felt like I was the biggest person out of my school friends, and at home. After I was abused as a child, this turned into self-hatred of my body, something I am still working through. As my anorexia developed, I really wanted to love myself or at least like who I was, but I didn't feel able to. I just felt so trapped. Eating disorders distort our perceptions of ourselves and when we start to realize this, it helps us to push back on those feelings.

It is *hard* though, and for most people who have experienced an eating disorder, your relationship with your body will always be a work in progress. While I definitely don't want to normalize a negative body image, because we should all be moving forward to acceptance, it's important to realize that struggling with your body image doesn't necessarily mean you are relapsing. It doesn't mean you are getting ill again, as long as you are coping with the mental health aspects around it in the best way possible. I do this through:

- Talking about how I'm feeling if I feel I need to.
- Getting dressed every day. What I mean is I don't just put on gym stuff or clothes that feel "safe" to wear, but actually put something on that makes me feel okay! Like me, I am sure you have clothes to cover up on "bad body days", but wearing these is not helpful – it won't actually make you feel any better.
- Washing my hair: maintaining good levels of hygiene are always important for me in recovery and they do impact how I feel.

- Being strict about not checking my body constantly.
- Being aware: notice when you are having a bad day and keep eating! Don't restrict because that will do more harm than good.

EXERCISE 7: IDENTIFYING YOUR FEELINGS

One of the first things that helped me realize there was so much more to my body image than just feeling ugly a lot of the time was linking back these feelings to my mood. Had something triggered me that day? Or was I just feeling so much it was easier to project those feelings into hating my body?

Have a look at the emotions wheel below. In the middle you can see the words "I feel...". Work your way around the wheel to find the words that best express how you are feeling. I know when I am really struggling emotionally, my body image gets worse. Now, instead of looking in the mirror and announcing to myself "I feel ugly", I think about what that actually means. What is wrapped up in that word "ugly"? Feelings of sadness, guilt... identifying these helps to give us the space to talk. When I worked this out, it felt so freeing and also helped with my communication too.

Body-Checking

This is when you constantly check your body to see whether it has changed shape. You might pull at parts of it, carry a tape measure round with you, see how far your hands fit around a part of your body. Throughout the depths of my anorexia, I spent a huge amount of time body-checking. I hated it, and I don't even know why I ever did it because it always made me feel so much worse and I now realize it is such a scientifically inaccurate way to measure appearance and there is so much more to me than this!

The more we body-check, the more we become fixated on certain elements of ourselves. Recently, I got a rash on my body caused by a viral infection. It kind of threw me a bit. It started as this mark on my side, and gradually spread all over my stomach, thighs and upper arms and made me feel self-conscious. Normally stuff like that wouldn't bother me, but over that period it made me really sad, to the point that I didn't want to get dressed and go out. We were in lockdown so it was pretty easy, but it frustrated me. I would put on a nice top for Zoom meetings, but straight after would get back into my pyjamas. A few days after it started, I was sitting on the sofa first thing in the morning messaging a friend, pretty much crying over how the rash was making me feel and how it looked. Then I felt guilty for being vain. I was in this strange cycle of feeling annoyed at myself for minding, but at the same time continuing to obsess over it. I sat there trying to work out why something that would normally just be a slight annoyance was beginning to take over my brain. Then I realized, usually I would be out and about speaking, running workshops, but right now in lockdown I had more time to scrutinize my body. Literally every ten minutes or so I was lifting up my top and staring at the rash, pulling it apart, hating it. Every time I looked at it I was feeling more and more horrible in myself. Plus, my stomach seemed to be growing every time I stared at it. I don't know if you have ever done anything like this, or whether right now while you read this you are grabbing at certain parts of your body. When I was at the height of my anorexia I would do this all the time, spend hours body-checking. I would imagine cutting out my tummy to try to get rid of it.

I don't have all the answers to body-checking, but for me it was about challenging it. Each time I had the urge to body-check, instead I would:

- Make a cup of tea
- Be intentional about doing something else
- Train myself to not immediately body-check when my hands weren't busy doing something else
- Distract myself

Eating disorders want us to look so inwardly at ourselves. They want us to focus just on us, our size, our shape, and just on the eating disorder. Sometimes it feels uncomfortable to push outwards, but the more we do it the easier it gets.

Is anyone else guilty of staring at their face during video calls? I know I am! I have a tendency to look at myself constantly. I don't even do it because I like what I look like, but to see what I look like and because I'm worried about what others think. When we are staring at ourselves a lot, those parts of us we struggle with look worse – we get fixated on them. One way to stop doing this is to switch your settings so that you can't see yourself or so that you appear smaller on the screen.

Changing Weight in Recovery

Your weight is likely to change during recovery and you will have to learn to navigate your new body. When you are having a bad day or week, or when you've noticed your body change shape, you might want to hide yourself and resort to wearing cover-up clothes such as joggers and hoodies! Don't get me wrong, there is a place for those clothes in our wardrobe, but it is so important that we make sure that we are wearing them for the right reasons. As you put on weight in recovery and your body changes shape, there are a few things that help:

1   Focus on the memories you have made since starting the road to recovery, and the energy you now have, instead of your size.
2   Get rid of old clothes: this might need a ceremony, it might need a grieving process, but get rid of the stuff that doesn't fit you, because it will only make you feel bad.
3   Buy some new outfits that make you feel good! Also see page 181.
4   Remind those around you that you might still be struggling. Have someone you are accountable to so that you can check in about your weight and how you are feeling if you need to.
5   Book some nice activities: I found this really important as I began to progress through my recovery. It helped to motivate me and meant I had less time to get fixated on my body.
6   Accept yourself and your past because it has made you you!

Sometimes in recovery we have to step outside the box and allow ourselves to dream. How many of you have stopped yourself doing something? Perhaps you have stopped yourself being naked with your partner or not gone out in the evening because you are struggling with your appearance? I know I have! And when I look back at this it feels sad. Sometimes we need to challenge ourselves to dream of those things we would do if we weren't afraid of our appearance! I know you will all be at different stages with this, but I wanted to share it as something to think about.

Social Media

I am sure there are a number of things that impact your body image – social media is a big one for me. Yes, I said it! I opened up that can of worms! On social media it is so easy to get into the habit of comparing and scrutinizing other people's bodies. Even if you watch videos online of people working out, you might actually not be watching them, but instead comparing your body! Does this sound like you? It is okay if it is, but how about we start to move forward from it?

TACKLING SOCIAL MEDIA

I spoke to Louisa Nicole Rose, a social media expert and campaigner, about her thoughts on social media and eating disorders.

She said: "Social media is overflowing with content that can have a negative impact on the way we see our bodies. Fitness accounts, fashion accounts, sun-kissed bodies and the latest food fads are just some of the types of content that are unregulated and often mindlessly posted. The flip side of this is that social media is also overflowing with the most wonderful and inspiring content that can boost our body image and mental health; content that promotes body positivity, self-love, self-care and openness. Surprisingly, you are in control of the content that you see. You just need to understand the algorithms that dictate what content appears for you. Which is easier than it sounds. Ultimately, most social media platforms want to ensure that the content you are served is content that you want to see; content that will entice you to stay and scroll that little bit longer. The way it determines what content will interest you is in part down to the data that you give it. Aside from the basic information entered upon signing up, platforms know what hashtags you click on, which posts you like/comment/share, whose accounts you follow, and who you're messaging behind the scenes. The more mindful you are about the information you're giving the platform through your behaviours within the apps, the more positive an impact this will have on the content that is served to you and therefore on your mental health."

Here are some of Louisa's top tips for dealing with social media:

1 Give yourself a "social media MOT" to make sure your social media behaviour is helping, not hindering your mental health.
2 If content you are seeing doesn't inspire or empower you or help you feel supported and valued, unfollow.
3 Set in app time limits so that you don't find yourself 64 weeks deep into an unhealthy social media account's posts.

4 Use in app discovery tools to discover new, interesting accounts for you. Follow hashtags on Instagram; explore discovery pages (e.g. For You Page on TikTok, Explore Feed on Instagram and Discover on Snapchat).

5 Consider your privacy settings. Going private can protect you from unwanted followers.

6 Post responsibly. The instinct to compare ourselves to others is nowhere more tempting than on social media so be the content you would like to see and don't convey a false reality.

7 If your mental health is suffering, I'd recommend a social media detox. Step out of the apps and focus on the present moment. Our state of mind can impact how we interpret content on social media, so be aware of how you're feeling and prioritize your mental health above all else.

EXERCISE 8: A POSITIVE BODY-CHECK

This exercise is going to feel quite challenging for some of you, and I totally get that. I also think we often believe that these sort of exercises should solve everything so we put so much pressure on ourselves to just do them and it will all be okay.

With this in mind, I would love you to go into it with an open mind. Body image can be so hard at times and feel impossible to crack but it isn't necessarily about fully loving yourself but being able to accept you for you.

Remember, you can include things like "I like my hair", or "I like my legs because they get me from A to B". Think about what your body does and all these amazing things it allows you to do.

Take some time to write three things that you like about your body. And then three things you like about yourself that aren't related to your appearance.

What I like about my body:

1

2

3

What I like about myself:

1

2

3

If you found that really hard, come back to it later on. Perhaps work through it with a friend. Sometimes it helps to have someone else to think about those other things with us.

Remember to take time for yourself after this, and journal if you found it hard.

Remember...

There is no denying it, our relationship with our body image can be really hard at times. It can throw us from the start of the day, and linger in our brains constantly nagging at us. Sometimes we try to push the feelings away, but it doesn't always work. Here are my key takeaways for you for those difficult days:

- Cut yourself some slack! You are going to go through different stages with your body image and that's okay. Some days will be harder and on those days do something kind for yourself.

- On bad body image days, do not restrict your food intake or punish yourselves with exercise because that won't help.
- Get dressed (and not just in jumpers and leggings).
- Book something nice!
- Remind yourself that what you see in the mirror isn't the reality. There is so much more to body image – start to unpack it, write it down.
- Next time you have a negative thought about your body, say something out loud and stop the thought progressing further. This might take a bit of practice and you might feel a bit silly the first few times you do it, but it will get easier. (This is becoming a theme of the book, eh? The more we train our brains, the easier things get!)
- Tell someone! I always text someone or tell someone that I am feeling a bit gross in myself. They can't fix it, but by telling someone it really helps.

I wanted to end this chapter with a letter to my body and I have left a blank spot under it in case you would like to do one too:

Dear Body

I am sorry for how much of my life I hated you. I am sorry that you carried around with you so much shame, guilt and feelings of disgust. I am sorry that you were tired so many times when I pulled you out of bed to go running and you were screaming for me to stop. I haven't fully accepted what shape you are and at times I know I can still say some really nasty things to you but I am thankful for so much. I am grateful that you have stuck by me, that you have helped me to get from A to B, you have kept me live and kept me going. I know that we have a long journey ahead of us but I know that together we can crack whatever life throws at us.

Thank you for holding me all those nights when things felt tough and for putting up with all I put you through. I am making a commitment to try harder with you. To try and show you more of how much I care about you.

Yours

Hope

Try writing a letter to your body:

CHAPTER 10

YOUR MENTAL HEALTH

Mental health difficulties are common and, thankfully, society is becoming more aware and accepting of them. I wanted to add this chapter in because so often we think about eating disorders and often forget they are mental illnesses. Like physical health, it is normal for our mental health to change and when it does, it is important to have coping strategies and a supportive network around you.

All mental illnesses deserve treatment and support, but it is important to remember that recovery from all of them is possible. And whatever illness you might have, it is not a life sentence.

In this chapter we are going to look at a variety of mental illnesses and how they can feed into eating disorders, and then look at how we can manage our wider mental health.

Common Mental Health Conditions

The following are some common mental health conditions that may occur alongside eating disorders:

ANXIETY DISORDERS INCLUDING GENERALIZED ANXIETY DISORDERS AND SOCIAL PHOBIA

Anxiety is a feeling of unease, such as worry or fear, that can be mild or severe. Everyone feels anxious at some point in their life and so anxiety in itself is not a form of illness but a normal physiological response. For example, you may feel worried and anxious about sitting an exam, or having a medical test or job interview. During times like these, feeling anxious can be perfectly normal.

However, some people find it hard to control their worries. Their feelings of anxiety are more constant and can often affect their daily lives. Some of the symptoms of anxiety include restlessness, feeling on edge, being irritable, tiredness, muscle aches and feeling sick. This may occur throughout the day or in specific settings, e.g. social gatherings.

The mainstay of treatment for anxiety disorders is psychological therapy, such as CBT, though in some cases medication can also be prescribed.

DEPRESSION

Depression is more than simply feeling unhappy or fed up for a few days. Most people go through periods of feeling down, but when you're depressed you feel persistently sad for weeks or months, rather than just a few days. The other core symptoms of depression are fatigue and an inability to enjoy previously pleasurable activities (anhedonia). Associated symptoms include poor concentration, impaired sleep and a lack of motivation.

Depression is not a sign of weakness or something you can "snap out of" by "pulling yourself together". It can be effectively treated predominantly with medication (depending on the severity) and various forms of psychological therapy.

SELF-HARM

Self-harm is when somebody intentionally damages or injures their body. It is a coping mechanism, and a way to gain control when everything seems chaotic. For some people it is a way of relieving tension, while for others it is a way of bringing emotions out when they have been feeling numb. People may self-harm in different ways, and for a specific reason or not. Self-harm can occur in a number of mental health conditions.

PANIC DISORDER

Panic disorder is an anxiety disorder where you regularly have sudden attacks of panic or fear.

OCD

Obsessive compulsive disorder (OCD) is a common mental health condition in which a person has obsessive thoughts and compulsive behaviours. Obsessions are unwanted thoughts that are difficult to shake off and can seem completely out of character, for example, the thought that you are a danger to others or that you are somehow contaminated. Compulsive behaviours are repetitive actions that are taken to diminish the distress caused by these thoughts, such as excessive handwashing, checking or cleaning.

CASE STUDY: BOBBY

One of the lesser known symptoms of depression is memory loss. Much of my past, in fact, is a mystery to me, particularly those times when my mental health was at its worst. Difficulties with focusing, making decisions, being present, confidence and emotional connection are commonly experienced by those living with mental illness. What I do remember is how living with depression shaped my young life. Many of my earliest memories are of masking behaviours, as I quickly learned that the adults around you feel more comfortable when you pretend to be happy. This swirl of locked-in emotions triggered a survival mode during

---

primary school. To get through each day without feeling totally overwhelmed, I distracted the loneliness by being with friends, the sadness by using humour, and the despair through escapism. One of the hurdles to sustaining this was that I hated myself. Thinking that I was innately wrong and was only liked because of the persona I had crafted. Either way, being liked for a pretend version of you holds no validation.

I also despised my appearance, thinking I was ugly to the extent I could hardly bare to look at myself. As I looked into mirrors, a Picasso version of myself looked back. Feeling out of control and more alone than ever, I would skip lunch to sit in the quiet sanctuary of the library. The escapism of books was a triumph to cling to.

Restricting my food intake gave me a feeling of safety, control and even success. I became "good" at anorexia when I felt bad at everything else. I had become adept at pretending everything was okay, so even convinced myself. When telling my parents I'd eaten out with friends or got something on the way home, they believed me. While I went on hating my body, society reinforced that slimmer was better. Meanwhile, I genuinely did not know men could have eating disorders, having never seen an example of this in the media.

While my diagnoses were ultimately not a surprise, the anorexia took longer to come to terms with. In fact, it was through long-term counselling and hosting early episodes of Mental Podcast that I first felt empowered enough to own this part of my story. With the help of supportive friends and family, I have found a strength through ongoing recovery that I never knew was possible.

My voice will stay raised for young people and all those struggling, through my campaigning for mental health education. The stigma will end and you'll see me kicking it *all the way. I am now proud to be the role model of a man overcoming an eating disorder that I needed but never knew existed.*

Eating Disorders and Wider Mental Health

It's really important to make a distinction between your eating disorder recovery and your broader mental health. When I was struggling with my mental health, I learned it didn't necessarily mean I was relapsing. In 2019 I'd had quite a bad year struggling with various things and as a coping mechanism I had worked pretty much 24/7. This wasn't healthy, or right! I ended up going back to my doctor and going into therapy (see Chapter 22). I realized over that summer that although mentally I might have been struggling, it didn't mean that I had gone back to my old coping mechanisms with food.

Emotional Responses

Many of us have an extremely emotionally fuelled relationship with food. Have you ever had an argument with someone and then gone straight to the fridge? Or after getting some bad news, reached for the biscuit jar or headed straight to the gym? This is an emotional response to an experience, and it is important to become aware of when you're doing it and choose to behave differently.

1   Ask yourself are you really hungry/do you really need to exercise?
2   Ask yourself are you doing it for the right reasons or to punish yourself?
3   Find a distraction: I find that journalling, watching a movie or going for a walk help.

This isn't an excuse to restrict what you are eating, but about moving to a space mentally where you can listen to your body and understand what you really need.

The same awareness is needed with body image. I find that my body image is so much worse when I am stressed, worked up or not that happy. Learning to make the distinction between your body and your feelings will stop you taking out how you are feeling on food and help you to stay in a positive space in your eating disorder recovery.

So, What Can You do to Manage Your Mental Health?

PRACTISE SELF-KINDNESS

On tough days it is even more important to be kind to yourself – to step back and practise self-compassion. I could write a whole book on self-care and exploring the relationship that I have with it, but the fact is even though it can be hard to be kind to ourselves on challenging days, this is when it is even more important that we try. Self-care doesn't have to be expensive or time-consuming – it can be as simple as drinking enough water or reading a book or getting some fresh air. I like to have a leisurely cup of tea, watch something on Netflix or write in my gratitude journal. I also think about what I might suggest to help a friend and remind myself it shouldn't be any different for me. Sometimes you won't feel able to do anything and that's okay; don't beat yourself up for that, but instead hold on to the fact that those feelings will pass. When you get to bedtime, it is okay to write off the day and start again afresh the following morning.

HAVE SOME KIND OF ROUTINE

Routine has been really helpful in my recovery – having a routine around meals, but also in my day-to-day tasks. This is a very individual thing, so plan what works best for you and, whatever your routine, make sure to work in certain times of the day when you can stop and settle.

DON'T PANIC!

I used to panic so much that I was relapsing when I had a bad mental health day. It is important to be aware of your feelings, but remind yourself that it doesn't mean you are getting unwell again. Check in with yourself, do something for you, try not to catastrophize your feelings, and speak out if you can.

STAY CONNECTED

Whether it's through having therapy or seeing friends, making connections is important for wellbeing. Work out who is in your support network and where you can go to for that additional help if you need it. Don't wait until a crisis to tell someone you are struggling.

MOVE!

Walking, stretching, exercise classes… whatever it is; if it's done in the right way, movement can be so helpful for our mental health. It is this that gives me headspace, helps me to readjust my thinking patterns and also allows me to work through things. I am going to talk about exercise more in Chapter 15 as I know that at times this can be quite a challenging relationship.

MEDICATION

I was terrified about going on medication, but I went on an antidepressant called citalopram for four years, and while the side effects for the first two weeks were hard, the long-term impact was amazing. It cleared the fog in my head, gave me energy to get through the day, and helped me to think broadly about what I could do to go to a better space. Not everyone needs to go on medication, but it certainly helped me. If you are worried about medication or feel you need to go on it, talk to your doctor. Remember, there is no shame in it. I chose to come off antidepressants when the time was right for me and it was hard reducing my dose, but I managed to do it with the right support around me.

Remember...

If you are struggling with your mental health, do make sure you reach out for support. I know this can feel really hard at times but so often we all wait until we hit crisis before asking for support and we need to remember that we don't need to wait that long. We deserve support and help so take some time to work out who you have in your life who can offer this support to you. See the Resources at the back of the book (page 239) for ideas on where to seek help.

CHAPTER 11

NEGOTIATING "DIET CULTURE"

Research studies show that dieting is linked to eating disorders, which is why I felt it was important to include this chapter, but I am by no means saying that eating disorders are dieting, or that every person who diets develops an eating disorder.

You may find this topic quite hard to grapple with. Like me, you might have been a serial dieter for years, you might have friends who appear to be constantly dieting... Whatever your relationship with dieting, I would like you to approach this chapter with an open mind and remember that as you read it the eating disorder might try and worm its way in, making you doubt yourself. If you get any of these patterns of thinking, please do become aware and make a note of them.

A Dangerous Culture

Diet culture affects all of us, but it has a particular effect on people with larger bodies, and those with eating disorders. It is hard enough for the average person, but for someone with an eating disorder eating less is the thing that made us really unwell, the thing that we can't do, but yet everyone is talking about it. Diet culture makes people think that being smaller is better and that certain body types are better. As a society, we seem so intent on commenting on someone's weight loss, instead of actually finding out what might really be going on for them.

Dieting has even begun to infiltrate political campaigns and public health work, which in itself is so frustrating. As I write this, we have faced months of lockdown due to COVID-19 and, again, diet has been there at the forefront, infiltrating every angle of life, creating this fear of putting on weight and making us self-conscious about our body shape and size.

We live in a society where talking about dieting is the norm; it is day-to-day chat that seems to be harmless, but it is far from that. People get sucked in and made to feel terrible about themselves and, having spent years trying different diets, get tempted to try a "new" one. But does dieting really ever make us that happy? Some of you might say, "Well, yeah it doesn't right this second, but it will do when I get to that size! When I get a bit thinner, lose a bit more weight..." We look at magazines, the media, social media, and we see these "ideal" bodies staring back at us – and let's not forget the targeted advertising. And then the crazes start... We convince ourselves that we should look the same.

Diet culture has created generations of people who are obsessed with their bodies. We spend hours scrutinizing ourselves because we believe that certain body types are "better" and that being thinner is "healthy". It isn't! What we are doing when we start dieting is turning off all the natural hunger cues that keep us alive. Perhaps throughout your whole eating disorder you have felt hungry and felt like a failure because of that. But being hungry doesn't mean you are failing – it is natural!

We need to stop congratulating ourselves on eating less and less. When those thoughts come into your head, find a way to stop them. I say something out loud to break my train of thought or tell someone close to me that I am feeling pressured to eat less. It can be particularly hard when friends or family are caught up in the diet culture too, constantly talking about it and discussing it. We need to try to be bold and push back. I know this is hard as it goes against everything the eating disorder might be telling us, but if we let it back in, it will slowly cause us to restrict again.

A CHANGING CULTURE

Before we get into the nitty-gritty of managing diet culture, I want to show you how diets and the way we view body shape has changed in the past 100 or so years. In the early 1900s, females idealized an hour-glass shape, then in the 1920s a slimmer physique became more popular. During the 1970s there was an increase in the number of slimmer models, then in the 1980s there was a move toward stronger, more athletic bodies. For some reason this didn't last long, and by the 1990s we had moved our focus back to being thinner. And by 2000 we reached a point where pretty much everyone had some hang up about their body. We saw an increase in people dieting, an increase in people finding fault with themselves. And then what? Yes, you guessed right! The diet industry swooped in and made us feel even worse about ourselves and our bodies. Yes, we have seen more changes as we moved through 2010s, but by this point so much of the damage had already been done!

A Quest for Happiness

Growing up I had been a serial dieter, constantly trying a new way to lose weight. Each month I would set myself new goals and I was convinced that the skinnier I got, the happier I would be. So many people feel this way, but I can sit here and 100% tell you that losing weight *doesn't* make you happy! When I look back at the young girl sitting on the beach in a hoodie, I feel so sad for her. Sad that she felt so trapped and so alone. Sad that she wanted to keep shrinking herself. What about you? What do you see when you look at your past history of dieting? What do you see in that individual?

I often think back to all those hours as a child, when I was so afraid to stop dieting because I was afraid I would overeat, that I would lose control without these rules in place. I wonder if you have felt like that. I wonder what dieting does for you. I wonder whether deep down you know that it is a silly thing to do, but perhaps you are reading this thinking, I am different from others, Hope, I *need* to diet! Or... let me get to the shape I want to be, *then* I will stop dieting. I know how hard it can be to give up the diet mentality – I was literally in it for decades – but moving on from it gives us so much more freedom and it allows us to trust our bodies again.

I believed if I dieted "better", then I wouldn't feel so bad. Maybe you feel like this or maybe like me, you know that dieting doesn't really work in the long term, but for so long you have clung on to the false sense of security it might have given you.

Or perhaps you know the facts, but you just hate what you look like and even in recovery this feels unbearable at times. Trust me; I know that feeling too well. But is this wrapped up in something else? I want to be really careful about making distinctions between dieting and eating disorders, but I know that sometimes when I feel tempted to diet, it is a guise for the eating disorder behaviour and rules to come back and infiltrate my life.

EXERCISE 9: YOUR RELATIONSHIP WITH DIETING

Take a few minutes to write about your relationship with dieting in the space opposite. Have a think about how dieting has impacted your life, and the fears you might have around stopping dieting. This will allow you to begin to call out the diet culture for what it really is, a money-making scheme which profits from people being told they need to hate themselves.

Here's my answer:

I spent so much of my life dieting. So much of my life hating myself, convinced that I could hate myself into loving my body. Trying diet after diet and failing a lot of the time. Feeling quite stuck and trapped in this thinking. Diet culture did this to me! Even in my recovery it made me start to dislike who I was. Told me that I wasn't thin enough to be loved. Made me preoccupied with appearance over other things that mattered so much more. I want to take a stand against diet culture right now! To realize I am worth so much more than it. To realize that my body has been through enough hatred and dieting never made me happy.

Now have a go:

Dieting "Rules"

The diet culture puts a heightened focus on calorie-counting and weighing ourselves. It tells us that we should be eating less and less, and counting more and more. It is a culture of numbers – we see them everywhere, on billboards, in supermarkets, in restaurants, on packaging... The message becomes that if you aren't losing weight, you are bad. We believe it; we allow the number on the scales so much power and allow it to dictate our mood for the entire day. Have you ever woken up in the morning (perhaps even today), weighed yourself and then realized that your weight has shifted a little? What do you think first? Is it that you had a bigger meal last night? Or you had something that you think was a "bad" food ... Does it then ruin your day? I have been there on numerous occasions and not only does the number always make me feel bad, but it dictates my feelings for the next day or two. I then barely enjoy eating anything that day and I spend the whole day body-checking and feeling self-conscious. A lot of this time, this slight change of weight is a natural fluctuation, maybe due to water retention!

Diet culture also has this tendency to name bad and good foods! We create this circle of guilt and shame when we eat something that is "bad" for us and then we either restrict, binge-eat or over-exercise. If we shift out of this thinking, it allows us to enjoy that food without feeling guilty.

Craving foods in recovery is normal, but diet culture makes this harder. When we are told to stop eating a certain food, we immediately crave it. We cut out carbohydrates and we crave bread, rice, pasta... I am sure you could complete this sentence with pretty much any food you cut out! What happens then is that we think about food for hours and hours, maybe nibble at it, put it back, feel guilty, have a bit more, then sit on the sofa feeling even more guilty. We then start going over and over it again, then make a new rule there and then telling us that we need to do "better". Do you get into this constant cycle of guilt, while always thinking about the food? I know I do.

A few years ago I cut out bread. Not for any specific reason, but just to gain back some control (or so I thought). I would order so much bread, it would sit in the freezer and every now and again I would toast it, eat the crust, and bin the rest. Firstly, what a waste of bread and, secondly, how ridiculous! Looking back, I should have had a slice whenever I craved it and made peace with the food. Then I wouldn't have thought about it so much or felt so guilty when I did eventually eat it.

But here is the thing, as soon as we start putting those rules on ourselves we create an unhealthy relationship with food, full of guilt and fear. We need to try to change our relationship with food in this way so that we aren't scared of it. Allowing ourselves to have it will help us to move on. If we move out of this state of depriving ourselves of food, we are able to slowly take steps to make peace with it because it is no longer emotionally charged. To move into this space of accepting foods, and allowing yourself all foods, you need to be curious about them. You need to start allowing them into your house, tasting them, and working out if you do actually like the food, and I don't mean telling yourself you don't (I have done that before and I am sure others have too).

EXERCISE 10: REFRAMING FOOD RULES

Food rules are everywhere, right?! We think if we eat X, we will be bigger the next day. Or if we eat X, we will lose control. Maybe these behaviours are still slightly wrapped up in your eating disorder and it has created the fear around certain types of food. This exercise is designed to help you tackle those rules.

In the left-hand column write a list of the rules that your brain has created, and in the right-hand column reframe that statement. I've given a couple of my own examples at the start.

MY "RULES"	REFRAMING
If I miss a day at the gym, I will put on lots of weight.	If someone else missed a day of the gym, it would have an impact and I am no different. In fact, having an extra day off when I need one is good for my body.
If I eat a bowl of pasta before bedtime, I will put on lots of weight.	If I eat a bowl of pasta before bedtime, I might bloat as my digestion may take a bit longer but that bloating feeling will pass.

MY "RULES"	REFRAMING

Remember...

You don't need to feel happy about your body the whole time, but it is important to move to a place of self-acceptance and lose the self-hatred. For me this was about beginning to know my own self-worth. This isn't easy and it takes time, especially when you have spent so much of your life hating your body and being brainwashed by diet culture.

To make the move away from diet culture:

1 Make the decision to move away from diet culture.
2 Throw out all your diet books and delete your diet apps!
3 Surround yourself with a good support network of people.
4 Diversify what you look at on social media.
5 Remember that everyone's bodies are different – we are all different sizes and shapes. There is no such thing as a perfect body!
6 Moving away from diet culture is a journey and will take time. Try not to beat yourself up if you fall back into old habits; but when you do, find a way to let them go.

I know for some of you reading this chapter might have been very difficult; there might still be so much fear wrapped up in giving up dieting. Or maybe you skim read it because it felt too uncomfortable. I am not going to pretend that challenging a diet culture and giving up a diet mentality is easy, but the result is an incredible, liberating freedom to eat what you want and enjoy it.

TOWARD A HEALTHY RELATIONSHIP WITH FOOD... FROM DR OBUAYA

The calorie-count does not fully represent the nutritious content contained within any given food. Numbers can also be unhelpful for someone who dislikes grey areas. Instead, focusing upon a food chart and ensuring that meals cover the food groups in a balanced fashion can ensure that a healthy meal plan is followed, rather than simply counting calories.

The "rules" associated with eating disorders are extremely controlling and rigid, but also confer a sense of safety. In the long term, keeping to these rules will be a barrier to growth and change. In order to truly move forward in your mind and body, you will need to start breaking some rules.

PART 3
DAILY LIFE

CHAPTER 12

SCHOOL, UNIVERSITY AND WORK

Whether you are still in education or at work, it can be hard to navigate your daily responsibilities and routine when you have, or are in recovery from, an eating disorder. What I'm sharing in this chapter is based on my own experience and it may not all work for you. Adapt the ideas as necessary to suit your situation and try to persevere until you find the daily support you need.

I spent my last year at school living in a mental health hospital, but a huge motivator for me was going to university. On so many occasions that helped me to push forward with my recovery. I was discharged from hospital two weeks before heading up to Birmingham University, where the support for eating disorder treatment was extremely limited. I took emergency food supplies – mainly cereal bars and other "safe" foods. I also took a cereal bowl from the hospital because I knew exactly how much cereal to pour in (although this bowl smashed six months in!). And, most importantly, I had a plan in place.

This was the plan I had devised from my time in hospital. A plan to eat exactly how many calories I had been having in hospital, to stick to the exercise plan I had worked out with Mandy, the nurse who had been running with me. It was extremely regimented but the reality of this was that I was terrified of what to do without it. I figured if I stuck to my exact same lifestyle with eating from hospital, then my weight would stay exactly the same, I would feel in control and feel okay. What I didn't realize when I had this plan, and perhaps some of you will relate to this, is that this makes life extremely limiting.

CASE STUDY: AMINA

When I was a teenager, I developed bulimia nervosa. Like many 14-year-olds, I told myself that I was not good enough. I became trapped in the cycle of bingeing and purging as a way to release the torrent of emotions that had built up over the course of several years. I was in high school at this point.

Often, I wanted to crawl to the back of the classroom and hide. I didn't want anyone to see me, I didn't want to be noticed. I didn't want them to see my skirt that was pinned and the dark spots around my mouth, which were still visible even after smothering concealer over them. They saw someone who was constantly on edge, fidgeting in her seat, and someone who wouldn't eat while her friends devoured their school dinners.

Being at school when I was struggling was a situation that I had to adapt to. I ate my lunch in an office, under the watch of a member of the wellbeing team, and then I was not allowed to leave the room for 20 minutes after. Lunch was only 40 minutes long to begin with, so by the time my 20 minutes had started everyone else was already in lessons. I was escorted to class – everyone stared at me as I walked in and there was the occasional remark shouted in front of the whole class. The teachers were told that I was strictly forbidden to be given a toilet pass after lunch.

I missed PE lessons if we were doing a long-distance run or were doing an activity requiring strength that I no longer had. I was questioned about whether I had eaten breakfast before I entered the sports hall. I struggled to get my head around why I was being singled out.

Being surrounded by people who didn't entirely understand what I was going through caused me a lot of anxiety. I was scared to use my time-out pass when I needed to, scared to ask to go to the toilet at other times, because of what the

*teacher would think. I was scared to walk into the canteen
and see people eating, worried about how I was going to get
from one lesson to another when I had no energy to climb up
numerous stairs. My mind was filled with anxiety surrounding
my eating disorder. It stopped me from reaching my full
potential; I didn't take part in extracurricular activities that
others were doing. My recovery was not linear – I had therapy,
I spoke to friends, I wrote poetry, and I eventually learned to
appreciate what my body can do.*

*My tip for those teenagers who are struggling with an
eating disorder at school is to reach out to others for support
– teachers, family, friends, professionals. Remember to keep
the conversation going and be honest about your emotions.*

Telling Others

If you are returning to education or work after having treatment,
think about whether you want people to know you are in recovery.
Would it be helpful or would you prefer to slot back in to avoid
having to answer too many questions? Bear in mind that if you had
been off with a physical illness, you would tell others and look for
their support – and it shouldn't be any different with a mental illness.

If you don't want to tell people, what is it you fear? I feared being
judged, work being taken from me, and that I wouldn't get a promotion.
But allowing ourselves to share some of our stories can really help.
Not only this, but it shows our real resilience in that we battle each
day and keep going! But maybe you are not sure if you actually want
to open up about your eating disorder yet and that's okay.

If you do feel ready to tell someone, I would recommend
identifying those who you trust and feel will support you, rather
than sharing everything with everyone. Give yourself time to find
the right people and then learn to talk to them... and, yes, I know
that is hard, especially if you have been let down in the past, but

please do give it a go. It helps to have someone to lean on and to be accountable to. It isn't about crying and having massive heart-to-hearts with everyone, but about letting a few choice people in. The more you can do that during recovery and build up a good support network, whether you are in education or at work, the better it will be for your day-to-day life.

EXERCISE 11: WRITING A LETTER

If you want to share your experience with someone, but don't know how to approach it, try writing a letter. The aim is to explain what you have been through, what would help you to move forward, and what support you need.

Think about:

- How much of your story you feel able to share.
- Anything specific you would like the person to know – for example, if it's someone you are likely to have lunch or dinner with, explain what meals or restaurants you find harder or easier.
- How the person can specifically support you day-to-day.
- The signs that you are struggling and what they can do to help you.

Once you have written this letter, try to give it to the person you've written to – if you can! I know it might seem a scary thing to do.

If you aren't quite ready for any questions that come from reading the letter, try ending it with something like:

"Thank you for reading this. I'm really glad I shared how I am feeling with you, but I don't feel ready quite yet to actually talk about it. Please give me some time. Thank you for being there for me."

Taking Time Off for Treatment

You might have had to take some time off for treatment, and this can be a hard thing to navigate. You might feel that people are judging your appearance, deciding whether you look like you need treatment at all. You might also feel they are watching your behaviour around food, which can make you panicky. Remember, you do not owe anyone an explanation as to why you are having treatment. We live in a society where people are so fixated on weight and food that, in effect, we have created a culture where disordered eating has become so "normalized", and it can be hard to try to recover in an environment where people are constantly judging us and our weight. When someone does comment, perhaps saying, "But you *look* healthy," remember that they don't mean it in a nasty way. Also remember the eating disorders twists all these words around in our heads, making it near impossible for us to trust what is being said.

It is also important to remember that time off for treatment can have other challenges when it comes to work – particularly if you feel you are missing out on things that are going on. Quite often with businesses the reality is it depends on how they see mental health. However, remember you don't have to disclose everything to your managers: choose how much you feel you would like to.

Whether you are in school, university or work, the best thing to do is to make a plan with your employer or teachers, so that you won't stress about what you might be missing. Work out with them how and when you want to be kept updated on what is going on.

Mealtimes

Eating outside of your home environment – whether it's in the school canteen, a staff room or a café near work – can feel hard and be confusing, so it is important to have a plan. My advice (at least to begin with) is to eat what you feel safe with at the same times each day.

During my first year at university my structure was very regimented. I survived by frantically calculating my pre-dictated calorie intake every few hours. My way of coping was hard work and time-consuming, especially when others didn't have or need the routine. I was always envious that no one else had such structure and rituals – they just *knew* what to eat. Also, how dull is calorie-counting?! Our life experience can definitely become limited by having intense food rituals, and because of them I certainly didn't have the best three years of my life at university.

If you are struggling with a new routine, how about sticking to X calories a day. When I used this approach, it meant I wasn't too upset if the times of meals changed, as the food I ate did not. I knew what I had to do to stay well and was determined to keep going with that.

I believe there is a time and place for routine and if you need that routine to keep well, don't feel ashamed about it, but you might want to gradually start challenging yourself – that's what I did in my second year at university. For example, maybe you could try having your lunch an hour later, or adapting your snacks slightly. By making these small changes, you can then start to build trust back in yourself.

EATING WITH OTHER PEOPLE

You might dread eating around new colleagues or classmates. You might feel they are all watching and judging what, and how much, you eat. The reality is that most of the time, no one is really looking at what we eat, even if our brains are telling us otherwise. If a communal lunchtime is hard, it is okay to take yourself away while you eat, or to have someone check in with you afterwards. You need to take care of your own needs and feel safe during your recovery. It's especially important to distance yourself from those people who tend to talk about food and dieting.

Something that I had to navigate when I first started working was going out for meals and drinks with the team, and to begin with I would just avoid them. If fear around social eating is the only thing stopping you going, it's important to step up and challenge that so that your eating disorder doesn't continue to dominate your life, even in recovery.

1 Work out what it would look like if you went to the social event. This will involve some mental planning. Who will you sit with? Who will be on hand if you are struggling or have you got someone to message if you need some advice? Thinking about the event and how it will look timing-wise will help you prepare for it. And then always have a plan in place afterwards just in case things felt harder at the event

2 Remember, you don't have to drink alcohol. Often peer pressure can be hard to ignore, even when people don't even realize they are doing it, but remember to take ownership of what works for you.

3 Ask to see the menu first if that helps. This is something that over time I would suggest you challenge and try to stop doing, but if it will help you go to something definitely, do it at the onset.

4 Be prepared for being triggered by other people's unhelpful attitudes to dieting and eating.

5 Be prepared for the eating disorder making you feel really awful the next day. I used to make sure I had some form of distraction prepared.

CASE STUDY: SALLY

"I can't believe you eat that! Do you know how many calories are in that?" I did know. Of course I knew. I knew the calories of every item in my kitchen cupboard. If I didn't know, then I wouldn't have been eating it. That was a bit of control I couldn't let go of for a long time.

Going back to work at a school after time off with anorexia was both an achievement and a huge challenge. We all had our lunch breaks at the same time. I could have hidden away in my dark and slightly damp office to eat, but then it would have been too easy to skip lunch. Instead, I had to push myself, to put myself out there among other people. And eat. With that came the awkward comments. Not out of spite, but because people didn't know what to say to a recovering anorexic who was now (very slowly) eating a two-finger Kit Kat.

I quickly realized that I needed to open up more to a few trusted people. They became my supporters at work, especially at lunchtimes. They were the ones who gave reassuring smiles across the table as I gingerly picked at food on those days when staying on track was hardest. They were the same people who would check in after meals if they could see eating had been an internal battle for me that day. They were the people who would say, "Well done," not in a patronizing way, but to acknowledge my achievement if they saw me eating something different, or if I shrugged off the comments from those who didn't know quite what to say.

My top tip for working while in recovery is to not be afraid to be vulnerable. In opening up to my colleagues I was able to ensure they had a clear perspective on what I was going through. At times I thought I had to be the person I had been before anorexia had broken me down, and I was afraid to show any weakness. However, in being brave enough to be vulnerable it meant people could support me, and meant my recovery continued while life got back to something like normal.

The World of Work

A work environment can be very challenging, from eating at your desk and feeling watched, to diet chat in the office, to work socials… If you feel able to, I would recommend talking to your manager. I know there will be some of you who feel afraid or worried about doing this, and you might prefer to just keep soldiering on, but I know speaking up does help. Looking back, there are times when I wish I had.

When I relapsed speaking up would have made it easier to deal with what was going on. I had such bad side effects from my antidepressants at first, and if I had told my manager, it would have given me more flexibility at work. I remember when it all got too much for me one day. I didn't feel able to tell anyone what was happening, so I went somewhere private and cried, and then put on a brave face and went back out.

The more we talk, and the more we open up, the better it is for us. Having these conversations can feel tough and awkward, so I want to share some things that might help:

- Remember that struggling with your mental health is no different to having a physical health condition and you don't need to feel ashamed.
- If you find it easier to begin with, send an email and book in a follow-up meeting. This might help you to get all your points across. You don't have to share everything – only what you want to.
- Emphasize that your condition does not have an impact on your day-to-day work.
- If you want to, ask a member of HR to attend the meeting too.
- Find out if your workplace offers any therapy, such as employee assistance programmes or wellbeing plans.

WORK LUNCHES

Triangle sandwiches (did I see your eyes roll?) – aren't they just the worst?! Like seriously, whether you have had an eating disorder or not, by the time you have lunch at a conference the sandwiches are slightly dry on the outside and limp on the inside! As you pick them up, they leave that sweaty marker on the tray… If it is a buffet lunch, remember you can take your own food to eat instead. If you are going out to eat, it is okay to ask where you are going.

WORKWEAR

You may find it really hard to know what to wear each day, and this isn't about vanity, but about not feeling self-conscious, which is such a horrid feeling. I had so many difficult mornings when I would get up, look in the mirror and proceed to try on everything in the wardrobe. See Chapter 17 for more on this.

REASONABLE ADJUSTMENTS

If you choose to disclose your eating disorder to your workplace, you may be eligible for some work adjustments. The 'reasonable adjustments' provision within the UK's Equality Act 2010 allows adjustments to be made in a working environment to allow you to continue with your duties without being at a disadvantage to your colleagues. This could be anything from flexibility around work hours, to dialling in to big meetings if you find being in large groups harder.

TRAVELLING FOR WORK

Right at the start of my recovery, I used to find travelling for work tough – the meals out, my routine changing, and not being able to exercise. If you have to travel for work, rewrite your routine for those days, allow yourself some slack around your emotions when travelling, and try to appreciate being away as much as you can.

FLEXIBILITY AROUND WORK

If no one knows what you are going through, it can be hard to get the flexibility you will sometimes need in recovery. It can feel impossible at times managing a condition that isn't chronic, but where you still have good and bad days. If I could go back in time, I would have come up with a plan with my manager to email her on those nights when I couldn't sleep (a result of my medication), and agreed some flexibility around working from home.

WHERE DO YOU FIND YOUR VALUE?

We spend most of our time at work and, if you don't feel valued, it can have a huge negative impact on your self-worth. At times when I wasn't valuing myself, I knew I might fall into my old habits of calorie-counting and exercising too much – things I knew I was so good at. We need to find value in ourselves and build our confidence so that we aren't reliant on what other people think. For me this came in the form of self-love, a topic that I believe runs throughout so much of this book. We spend so much time worrying about what others think, when actually it would be better to focus on who we are and the skills we have.

This is something I have to navigate constantly, working as a freelancer in a world where social media dominates everything – where we measure other people's lives through what they tell us in their feeds. We need to make a conscious choice to focus on ourselves instead of making comparisons, and this gets easier the more we do it.

The next time you walk into the classroom or the office, perhaps instead of immediately comparing yourself to others, instead of allowing your brain to tell you that you shouldn't be there, that you are less good, less pretty, more of a failure than others, how about instead choosing to ignore that voice and realizing the impact you have!

EXERCISE 12: MENTAL HEALTH ACTION PLAN

Think about what you really need to happen in your education establishment or workplace to support your mental health and recovery.

1   What can your organization do to support your wellbeing?
2   What things might trigger you, especially at certain events or certain times of the year?
3   What are the early warning signs that you might be struggling that your manager and supportive colleagues or classmates should be aware of?
4   What do you fear may happen by you sharing this (e.g. work being taken from you)?
5   What actions can you and your manager or teacher take if you feel like things are getting difficult?

Remember, the more information you put in the better!

Think about sharing your plan with your work friends, manager, teacher – whoever it is you rely on for support. If it feels too hard to share all of it, try to pick out something that would make a big difference to you – for example, letting people know you need information about restaurants and menus before a social event.

Top Tips for Recovery During School, Work or University

- Try to generate some sort of routine, from the very start of the day.
- Have at least two days off from exercise each week.

- Whatever your school or work schedule, try to eat three meals and three snacks every day. Over time you will be able to make changes and eventually take on a week-long approach, instead of working to a day-to-day schedule.
- Remember that your feelings about food are in your head and not your reality.
- Remember your motivations for wanting to stay well.
- Remember how your eating disorder ruined your life and don't let it spoil your experience of education or work now.
- Don't beat yourself up if you have a bad day – it doesn't mean that your recovery is over.

COMMUNICATION WITH YOUR EMPLOYER... FROM DR OBUAYA

Massive strides have been made in recent years in reducing the stigma around mental health issues in the workplace. You are certainly not obliged to go into great detail about your full eating disorder history with your employer, but letting them know that you are in receipt of professional help can help your employer to make reasonable adjustments to support you.

Many people worry about the impact of disclosure on their employment. You are protected against discrimination by various forms of legislation, including the Equality Act 2010.

Key Takeaway: Focus on what you want to achieve in your education and work, and don't let the eating disorder stop you.

CHAPTER 13

CHRISTMAS

When most people think of Christmas, they get excited about the thought of the food, alcohol, Christmas parties... For many, having a ready-made excuse to eat and drink as much as they want is ideal. For those with an eating disorder, this excitement is often replaced with a feeling of dread. For me, the anticipation and anxiety of Christmas used to kick in around October. By the time November rolled around and I'd answered the dietary requirements questions for celebratory lunches, and booked my place at the Christmas dinners, the fear had really started to kick in:

"What if I don't eat enough?"

"What if I eat too much?"

"Are people going to watch what I eat?"

So many questions suffocating me... sound familiar?

We live in a society where there is a big focus on food events throughout the year, and Christmas can feel like endless family gatherings (with food at the centre), causing panic for people living with eating disorders, however far through their recovery they are. And, of course, we gather with family and friends we may not have seen for a while. They think it is totally okay to make comments about weight and appearance and your eating disorder quickly translates "You're looking really healthy" into "I look really fat" in the blink of an eye.

Despite all this, getting through Christmas does not have to be hard, and surviving – and even enjoying it – is 100% possible. I am living proof of that!

My Memories of Christmas

Each Christmas throughout my teens was the same: stress about food, avoiding eating as much as I could, and then making up for the fact I had eaten lunch by making myself sick. On my last Christmas before I went into hospital, we got up early and opened our Christmas stockings – it was always so much fun to do that. I went for a run and opened more presents when I got back. Then I picked my way through a dinner, knowing that my parents would be watching, fully aware of what was about to follow. I was so naïve back then, and I was still best friends with anorexia. I loved how "she" made me feel and loved that even at a time like Christmas when I really struggled, she seemed to be there for me.

Little did I know that 11 months later my heart would nearly stop, and I would be admitted to a mental health hospital, where I would spend a year recovering. But during that Christmas in 2005, I didn't care. I didn't care about the strain on my family, the upset and the tears. I didn't care that I probably made everyone's Christmas so much worse. No, none of that mattered as long as I kept pleasing my best friend, anorexia. She made me feel good, reassuring me when life seemed so rubbish.

After I came through my relapse in 2016, I wanted to have minimal stress around food and Christmas, so I took control of the situation. For me this involved hosting Christmas, being hands-on with the food, and reminding myself why I wanted to stay well. Cooking Christmas dinner for my family, eating it, and actually enjoying eating it was a huge step forward in my recovery; a step that I was proud to take.

EXERCISE 13: REWRITING THE RULES

Those with eating disorders often create "rules" for themselves and perhaps even more so around events such as Christmas.

Use the chart below to think about what rules you have in place and then try rewriting them. By doing so you can call them out and be in a strong place to realize they are rules you made up! I've put examples of ones that came up for me at Christmas and how I rewrote them.

Think about when each rule comes up and what triggers it. This is an ongoing exercise that can be used at anytime, not just at Christmas. Rewriting the rules is a way of training your brain – over time the rules will shift and become more natural to break away from.

EXISTING RULE	REWRITING THE RULE
Whatever I eat on Christmas day is worse than other days.	What we eat at Christmas is not any different to what we normally eat; and just because it is Christmas, that doesn't mean the food is worse or will have a different impact on us.
Sitting around watching TV at Christmas is really bad for me.	Resting sometimes is really important to allow our bodies to repair.

EXISTING RULE	REWRITING THE RULE

The Support of Loved Ones

Perhaps at Christmas more than at any other time, we need to be honest about what we need. Here are some things people said to me that I found helpful. See also page 77, What to Say to Your Loved One.

"IT WILL BE OKAY"

When I began hosting my first Christmas meals, I found them challenging. I felt suffocated by all the food that was around and so scared of eating too much or too little. Those four simple words, "It will be okay", helped to defuse my mind when it was going off on a massive tangent. They helped to break the cycle when I was staring at a plate of food, worrying about the calories I was about to consume. They interrupted that anorexic voice in my head and helped me come back to the room.

"I AM HERE IF YOU NEED ME"

This statement goes a long way to helping us not feel like a burden to others. I know I sometimes feel so bad when I struggle at what should be a really nice happy time for everyone. It is when I feel bad about it that I stop talking.

"I KNOW CHRISTMAS CAN BE REALLY HARD AND THERE IS LOTS OF FOOD AROUND, BUT YOU DON'T HAVE TO EAT IT ALL"

This may seem like a silly thing, but seriously it is such a good reminder for someone in recovery. The amount of food around at Christmas, and the expectation to eat loads, is at times hard. So this small reminder helps us feel in control again.

"LET'S GO AND STRETCH OUR LEGS"

A healthy walk on Christmas Day is never a bad thing and for those of us who may struggle with exercising compulsively it does help.

"I KNOW THIS IS HARD FOR YOU, BUT WE CAN TALK ABOUT IT AFTERWARDS"

The acknowledgment that Christmas isn't easy helps us to talk about it.

"IT'S ONLY ONE DAY – HOLD ON IN THERE!"

Yes, and as patronizing as this sounds, it is one day and you can do this. We can do this together. We can manage our eating disorders and get through it. It might be hard and feel like a struggle, but once we have done it we can be so proud of ourselves and then have an easier day on Boxing Day.

Top Tips

- Have a plan in place for Christmas Day. Book in a call or meeting with the people you are spending Christmas with to work out what meals are going to look like on the day.
- Make sure your plan includes self-care/me time.

- If you know of a family member who will be there who likes to talk about diets and weight, ask someone to have a private word with them.
- Have a response in place in case someone says something that you find hard and triggering.
- Have a distraction plan in place if things get challenging; this could be stepping away from the mealtime once you have eaten, going for a walk or playing a board game.
- If you are worried about the food on the day, plan back-up food.
- If you have someone who attends that always watches what you eat, someone who might ask about your eating disorder and make it difficult, make sure you sit somewhere else.
- Don't put too much pressure on yourself to have a good day.
- Remember, it is just one day!

PREPARE AND PLAN... FROM DR OBUAYA

Christmas and other significant anniversaries may feel like daunting prospects and dates to dread, particularly if traumatic past experiences are associated with these dates. However, there is an opportunity to prepare for these events and put in place plans to minimize stress and anxiety that may predictably otherwise arise.

It is also worth planning in advance a review consultation or session with key members of your professional (and personal) support network to strategize appropriately together.

Key Takeaway: Remember to do you. Find out what will help you have the best possible day with the least stress around food.

CHAPTER 14

DINNER PARTIES AND EATING OUT

An invite to eat out or go to someone's for dinner is a really positive thing for most people, a natural and enjoyable part of their social life. When you have an eating disorder, this seemingly "simple" activity can be a minefield. In this chapter, we are going to look at some of the things it might trigger and how to deal with them.

For so long, I got so anxious about going to dinner parties and eating out. It used to make me so frustrated. I'd think, "Why do people like sitting around a table to talk and eat? Can't we just catch up with drinks?" I used to make up excuse after excuse as to why I would need to arrive just after the meal had finished. When a meal couldn't be avoided, I would spend the entire time frantically adding up all the calories, working out exactly what was going into my body, hating the whole thing, and feeling so unsure. I would then become stressed, weighing up whether it was worth it for the amount of guilt I felt afterwards. Sound familiar?

As I began to start recovering and felt able to eat out more, I then had to navigate meals out with people who might have their own issues around food and dieting.

CASE STUDY: ISA

Hosting and attending dinner parties is now one of my most favourite things. I'm not talking about anything majorly fancy, but there's something wonderful about Friday night rolling around, buying a bottle of relatively cheap wine, and turning up at a friend's house for dinner. I love the smell of something delicious cooking, the dancing tea lights on the table, and the sound of a good Spotify playlist. The taste of the first sip of wine and inevitable glorious combo of chips and dip that mark the turning from week to weekend.

I've had a whole load of things served up at dinner parties, ranging from a good solid ready meal and peas, to Thai green curry with rice and naan, chicken fajitas and fancy things like Ottolenghi chicken that had been marinating for two whole days. The food is good, actually usually the pudding is better, but the most important thing is it's not really about the food at all. It's about the clinking of glasses, the catch-ups, the singing into wooden spoons as the night progresses, and having what I like to call sunshine moments with the people I love.

It hasn't always been this way, though. Back in my teens, I felt a sense of crippling anxiety toward dinner parties. What time would the food be served? What would it be? What ingredients would they use? What portion would I be served? Would there be alcohol? I've always been an inherently social person, but the whirlwind of these thoughts definitely impacted my ability to be present in the moment, and to see the dinner party as more than the food.

Making peace with food, learning that food is essential to allow my body to function, but also that food is supposed to be deliciously satisfying, has allowed me to reclaim these occasions which offer me so much more richness and colour in my life. It really helped me to acknowledge that no one food can make or break my health, and that the stress from worrying about food does so much more damage to my body than any one food could ever do.

Of course, not every dinner party I attend is the best night of my life, and sometimes the food is incredible and sometimes it's distinctively average. Sometimes, I still find myself getting home and needing some toast. It's all okay! We're all just human. The point is, the social connection, the discussion, the memory making, the laughter, actually that might be more aligned with our true values than the perfect plate may ever be. And just to clarify, the perfect plate doesn't exist anyway.

If going to dinner parties is something that feels challenging, I would definitely recommend bringing this up with your psychotherapist or registered nutritionist/dietitian. A great way to start can be by practising at home, having someone in your household "host" a dinner party, starting with a meal you know you are okay with. Then you can build on this, working up to dinner at a friend's and so on and so forth. Notice where the eating disorder rears its ugly head, and develop some tools to help manage it when it does. Over time, it does get easier. It can also be helpful to acknowledge that the eating disorder wants to keep you isolated all for itself, and focus on the bigger picture of leading a richer and more meaningful life.

EXERCISE 14: CHALLENGING YOUR THOUGHTS

Write down all the automatic thoughts you have around dinner parties. Do this in the first column – and in the second column write the alternative rational way of thinking about it. Be as honest as you can be and feel free to include any fears that you might have. I've given you examples.

THOUGHT	RATIONAL THOUGHT
If I eat out tonight, I will put on loads of weight.	If my friend ate X, they wouldn't change shape so why is it any different for me?
If I eat in X restaurant, there will be nothing on the menu I like, then I will feel guilty and have to compensate.	No one else would compensate for eating something so I don't have to. I need to be curious about the menu, try something with a different flavour or order a few different dishes.
If I eat X, then everyone will think I am okay and totally fixed.	I can explain to people that I can enjoy the meal and still be finding it hard.

Top Tips

PLAN AHEAD

Finding out as much as you can about the meal you are going for will reduce your anxiety. When I first came out of hospital this was about knowing where we were going, looking at the menu, identifying the safe foods I could have, and then knowing roughly what time we would be eating.

BE WITH PEOPLE YOU TRUST

This can be hard at times, particularly if it is a work function, but where possible identify someone who you can turn to for support, if necessary. If you are attending a buffet and you haven't got that person with you, pick someone in the room and copy what they have on their plate. If there isn't anyone that you feel you can do that with, have your phone to hand in case you need to text someone. At the beginning of my recovery, I would often send a picture of my plate or the menu to someone to check in with. These are habits that you won't want to get fully fixed on, but as a short-term plan they will help you to gain more confidence and trust in yourself.

SPEAK UP BEFOREHAND

If you have someone there that you trust, tell them beforehand that you might find this hard, and ask them to look out for you looking distracted or sad.

PLAN TO MAKE MEMORIES

Focus on the memories that you are making, instead of counting your calories!

Challenge Yourself

About five years into my recovery I gradually pushed myself out of my comfort zone and felt able to go to a dinner party without asking what was going to be served and, while it felt uncomfortable at first, it got easier over time. By gradually pushing myself out of my comfort zone, I've now reached a stage where I'm okay just turning up to things.

When you feel ready, why not speak to a friend or family member that you trust and ask them to plan a dinner party. If you need to the first time, allow them to talk you through the cooking and food. After that, try to ask less and less about what will be on the menu, what time you will be eating, etc.

This could be a great challenge to set yourself every fortnight. Make sure you have time to debrief after and record your feelings in your journal. Remember that the feelings might set in the day after (I always have something fun planned to distract myself).

CASE STUDY: VERITY

I had developed an eating disorder in my teens. In my twenties, I remember a time when everything I planned socially would be accompanied by feelings of panic about being in a situation that potentially involved food and how that would affect things. There were a few select friends who knew about my eating disorder and therefore I could ask them and check if food may be part of the plan, but there were some who didn't know. I would then think in my head of all the things I could say: "I've already eaten" "I'm not that hungry actually," or "I'm going to eat later." It was exhausting and stressful.

I had grown up Christian, although I had lost my way for many years. I came back to faith and started attending church with regularity in my mid-twenties. I wanted to be part of the community. However, as many may know, church gatherings can involve food and eating together! Therefore, I began to withdraw and miss out on social events and meeting new people. I would find myself making up excuses as to why I wouldn't be able to make it for the meal part, but could come after.

In my late twenties, when I wanted to be part of a new church that was starting, I eventually plucked up the courage to reach out to the vicar. I will never forget the kindness of this vicar and his wife who listened to me and took my issues with food on board. To break the silence and secrecy by speaking up about my eating disorder was one of the most important choices I made. They would check in with me when gatherings were happening and let me know if there was food and what it would be. There were times when I would decide not to come for the food part and no pressure was put on me. Other times, they kindly made sure I was catered for with my "safe" foods. They would also meet with me one on one to talk and pray. I was so grateful and such support gave me hope and encouraged me on my journey to recovery.

Having selected people I knew I could trust to be accountable to was invaluable. I knew these people were there for me, cheering me on even in the toughest of times. It helped to be able to share what was happening to me or to share the things I was anxious about, as well as when they challenged me to keep going when I felt defeated. To break the silence and secrecy and tell someone was an important step.

DON'T TRY AND SECOND-GUESS...
FROM DR OBUAYA

However uncomfortable you may be feeling in social settings, your friends, family and acquaintances will most likely be feeling the same way. It is difficult to know what to say to someone who is struggling with an eating disorder and there is a tendency to err on the side of caution, so as not to cause offence, but this can create an awkward atmosphere. It is best not to second-guess what people are thinking: do not assume you are being judged, many people simply struggle to find the right words. Humour can be a good ice-breaker in such situations!

Key Takeaway: Be curious. Many of us may have forgotten what it is actually like to eat something we like – we'll choose something that is "safe" or something that we have had before (even if we don't really like it). So this week, when you go out for dinner I challenge you to be curious. Try something new, allow the taste to land in your mouth. And when you feel yourself perhaps panicking that evening, or the next day, trying to add up the calories in your head, instead focus on those memories you made that evening.

CHAPTER 15

EXERCISE AND PHYSICAL ACTIVITY

Before we start this chapter, I would like you to complete this sentence:

I exercise because _____

Be really honest with yourself. Do you exercise because you want to? For enjoyment? Or deep down is it because you feel pressure to? Perhaps you get itchy feet if you aren't able to go out and exercise. Or perhaps you are stuck in a bit of a cycle with exercise.

For someone with an eating disorder, exercising can be a complete minefield. I am not sure whether you exercise now or how it makes you feel but, if you are thinking of starting to exercise again, have a think about how that might look. It is important to add here that if you have a clinical team, talk to them before you start an exercise programme. I was able to do this when I was in treatment and it really helped me change my thinking around working out. Be aware that it can take time to get to a point where you have a healthy relationship with exercise.

My Exercise Journey

The reasons I run have changed massively over the course of my life. My relationship with exercise started out when I was at junior school. I was always quite good at running and, back then, I exercised for the right reasons.

A few years down the line, the exercise began to take over. The anorexia began controlling my every move and what used to be something I loved, gradually became something I *had* to do.

I was in denial about my exercise obsession, as well as the anorexia diagnosis. When I attended CAMHs in Bristol and my mum began monitoring my eating and exercise regime, I thought they were trying to make me fat and that they were jealous of how good I was at exercise. I carried on with what I knew how to do best.

One of the hardest parts of my recovery has been the exercise. During my three years at university I ran every day, even if I had been out the night before. I trained for the London Marathon when I was aged 20 and ran myself into the ground with overtraining. Exercise was my way of coping with a bad day and I knew that at some point I would need to tackle it.

In April 2014, I decided to see if I could train for a marathon without losing weight and becoming obsessed with exercise. Everyone around me thought this was stupid, and they spent the months before the marathon worrying constantly. But in April 2015 I completed the Brighton Marathon with a new personal best. I could never have done this had I worked out too much, or not eaten enough.

During my training someone said to me you wouldn't choose not to put petrol in your car before a long journey, so why would you choose not to eat before exercising. I began to understand that food is fuel.

So I know now that despite exercise and running being a massive part of my illness, it is a massive part of my recovery as well. Recovery for me isn't about never exercising again, but it is about doing it in a healthy way. Now I run because it gives me the headspace to think about things; it has transformed my recovery from anorexia, and has allowed me to understand my body and the power for fuelling.

Recently I started running a few times a month with a group of people, led by a coach called Andy Smith (www.andysmith.com). He got us to do some drills, one of which was focused on Mindful Running. We had to run slower and listen to our breathing and tune in to our body. At first, I really struggled with it. My mind told me that I wasn't burning enough calories and that this was a waste of training. I found it uncomfortable and there was no denying that, but I pushed through that thinking and kept listening to my body, and I found the wellbeing aspect amazing. What it did was it allowed me to reset my body in such a way that I was able to tune in with how I was feeling, and how my body was in itself.

The other exercise which really helped was using a metronome. I set it on my phone in a way that I can then breath alongside it. For me, running was so tied up with speed. So, going back to these basics and learning to listen again helped me to get into a better headspace. Then exercise can become a time that we use to check in with ourselves, and use the time to reflect and recharge, rather than pushing ourselves.

CASE STUDY: LAURIE

Deep down, I'm a lazy person. I'm not proud of the laziness, it's not a part of me that I willingly flaunt or advertise. Maybe its origins lay in the weekly ritual my family would have of forcing us to walk around yet another loch (living in the Highlands of Scotland meant we were never in short supply of inspiration, annoyingly) or perhaps I just really like sitting down. My dissatisfaction with my body and the spiralling grip I had on aspects of my life combined forces to finally topple the dominance that laziness had held over me for so long. I was entering a period of my life, adolescence, where my physical appearance suddenly held a currency previously invisible to me. My relationship with exercise is fraught to this day, even in my current state of "recovery". We're bombarded with aspirational images and made to believe that, no matter our shape, we're insignificant. I try my best to temper those external voices and focus on my own internal one. It's a long process, but when it comes to exercise, I try to find a balance between my expectations and the realities of my condition.

Unhealthy Exercise

The difference between exercise being healthy and unhealthy is our motive for doing it. So often people exercise to "earn" food, to "allow" themselves something to eat or to punish themselves. This takes all the fun out of exercise and instead pushes us to a place where we feel we *have* to go, and as a result we stop listening to our body and what it needs. Exercise addicts will find time no matter what – whether it means missing school, taking time off work, showing up late, or not at all, to social engagements or planned activities, working out when they are tired or have an injury, or perhaps in their room secretly. The thought of not working out fills them with fear and dread.

Not only might you experience side effects mentally from an unhealthy exercise regime, but there are also physical side effects such as Relative Energy Deficiency in Sport (RED-S) syndrome. You may stop ovulating and menstruating, get stress fractures or irreversible osteoporosis – and in extreme cases people can die of over-exercising.

EXERCISE 15: WHAT'S YOUR RELATIONSHIP WITH EXERCISE?

You might be reading this, thinking you exercise enough, maybe even more than others, but that you don't have a problem with it. Or perhaps you justify it by saying it is a ritual you have to do. With this in mind, I want to ask you some questions:

1 Do you constantly think about exercise and your next session?
2 Have you missed social activities in the last two weeks so that you can go to the gym?

3 In the last month, have you not allowed yourself time off even when your body has been feeling really tired?
4 Have you stopped enjoying the majority of your exercise sessions?
5 Do you feel angry if you aren't able to exercise for a day?

If you answered yes to more than two of these, than I would suggest seeking help from your doctor or someone close to you. A doctor is a really good starting point and they will be able to signpost you to other services. Another option would be to speak to a nutritionist.

EXERCISE 16: TRYING SOMETHING NEW

I want you to set aside your usual exercise routine and do some fun movement that isn't at all punishing.
You could:

- Sit and stretch.
- Go for a walk and really notice your surroundings rather than going at a fast pace.
- Book a class with a friend and focus on having fun.

Now add your own ideas.

Top Tips

BE ACCOUNTABLE TO SOMEONE

Do you have someone that you trust and that you can be honest with? Let this person know the warning signs of you starting to exercise too much and ask them to challenge you if they notice them.

PROFESSIONAL SUPPORT

I see a personal trainer every six months. She has helped to change my thinking around exercise and I've become stronger in my body and as a person. Getting that professional support if you are returning to exercise can be really helpful. Make sure you do your research and make the person aware of your history. This is important so that you don't exercise for the wrong reasons and keep it at a healthy level.

CHECK IN WITH YOURSELF

Keep checking in with yourself about why you are working out. Are you doing it to punish yourself? Or because you want to? Can you have rest days? These check-ins are essential and if you don't feel able to have them, it's important to address why that is. If you feel overly anxious when you aren't able to work out, it is important that you immediately have some time off. This will allow you to go back to the basics with exercise and help your brain to settle again. This will feel really uncomfortable, but distract yourself, keep yourself busy, and when you are ready, try to reintroduce gradual exercise again. Make sure you have people around you who can support you through this.

FUEL

Fuelling yourself is key. If we don't fuel ourselves adequately, we won't work out as well. I am testament to this. Turn to

Resources (page 239) to find where to get some solid nutritional advice.

INCLUDE SESSIONS WITH FRIENDS

Fun training sessions with friends help to stop me getting obsessed again. If you don't feel able to do this kind of activity, then perhaps it is a sign that you need to have some time off.

IDENTIFY YOUR TRIGGERS

For example, if you find cardio machines in the gym triggering, avoid them. I don't use Strava because I know I might get obsessed with my running distances, keep comparing my training with what others are doing, and then become competitive in an unhealthy way. Identifying these triggers and working out a healthy way of managing things is so important.

CLOTHING IS SO IMPORTANT

You might think it sounds vain, but if you are going to the gym or running and you feel body conscious, it might make your brain backtrack into a worse situation, putting pressure on yourself to work out more.

Key Takeaway: Everyone's use of exercise in recovery looks different and it is important to work out what works for you. Stay focused on yourself rather than comparing your workouts with other people's. Take time getting to know your body again, keeping and checking in with yourself, and have a support team in place.

THE CHALLENGE OF EXERCISE... FROM DR OBUAYA

Getting exercise right is a big challenge, as there can be a lot of guilt associated with undertaking strenuous activity and yet we know that there are many mental health benefits from movement and exercise.

If in doubt about what the right amount and type of exercise is right for you, do seek help from someone suitably qualified to assess your needs and provide advice.

CHAPTER 16

DATING AND LOVE

Dating can be difficult at the best of times – from the small talk to dating etiquette – but there is a whole new set of challenges when you have an eating disorder.

I always found dating stressful and it triggered an awful internal dialogue: "Do I tell them I have an eating disorder?", "What will they think? Will they still like me?", "What if I freeze when I look at the menu and can't find anything I like the look of?", "Will they judge my appearance?"

In the world of dating, it feels like food is everywhere. I found this frustrating and stressful, and I had to start taking control, choosing where we went and what we had to eat, or try to plan dates that didn't revolve around food.

Then, of course, if you start dating someone successfully, you move on to meeting the family – cue more feelings of judgement and more anxiety. "What will they think?", "What will they say?", "Whose job is it to explain about my issues around food?"

My Story

When I got admitted to a mental health hospital, I had been dating someone for a few months. He was lovely, very patient and kind. He had gone to university and just before my admission I went to stay with him. I vaguely remember that my sister had called him to tell him what was going on and I was so annoyed about that. I didn't feel like it was anyone else's business as it was up to me to own my story; but I think part of me also didn't want him to know because it meant it would be easier to hide what I was feeling. I arrived at his university and although I was exhausted from the train ride I was determined to be fun. But my mind would wander to food, calories and exercise and I couldn't stay focused on anything he was saying. I wasn't even remotely interested in his friends. A few weeks later I was admitted to hospital and he came to see me. I was allowed out for a few hours, but told that under no circumstances could we be intimate because of my weak heart. I felt so embarrassed that this was even a thing. We went to Sainsbury's to get a snack and I couldn't find the exact bar I normally had. I had a meltdown because the one that was there had a few more calories. Afterwards I felt so sorry for this guy and to this day I feel like he was completely out of his depth with me. Not because he didn't like me or care about me, but just because I was so trapped in my illness. I soon realized I wasn't well enough to date and the relationship ended.

Dating in recovery was difficult, mainly because I didn't want to slip up. I wanted to push myself and to start living a bit more, but was so afraid of what people would think.

EXERCISE 17: ARE YOU READY TO DATE?

Maybe you are dating at the moment, maybe you are too afraid to date, or maybe you date but then self-sabotage. I have been in all three of these situations and it can feel really tough at times, especially at different points in recovery. Before we unpack this in more detail, I want you to try answering the following questions: ·

1   What are your core beliefs? Are you comfortable with who you are? Or are you dating to seek approval from someone else?
2   How do you feel letting someone into your fold?
3   Are you dating because you want to for you or because you want to be accepted by someone?
4   Do you feel able to remove yourself from the eating disorder further so you can get someone else to make the distinction between you and the illness? Even when in recovery, there is the potential for there to be three people in the relationship (you, your partner and the eating disorder) and this won't make the relationship okay.
5   How does dating make you feel?
6   Do you have the brain space for a relationship or are you still thinking about food all the time?

Hopefully these questions will help you work out whether you are ready to date or whether you need to spend some time on yourself.

Be aware of whether you're dating for yourself and not to fill a hole in your life. All my past relationships were like that and I am finally in one where I am accepted for me. Where my partner knows how to support me and how to hold my hand on those tough days. I also know that my self-worth is found in myself and not in my partner, but it is a work in progress and it is important that you work out when you are ready for it.

Relationship Difficulties

Some issues you may come across when dating in recovery include:

SELF-SABOTAGING

Sound familiar? I was sure that whoever came along was going to leave me, so I pre-empted it and pressed the destruct button. The anorexia would often tell me I wasn't worth anything, that no one would really love me, that I wasn't valued or enough for anyone. Because I believed it, I would then self-destruct. There will be times in your relationships when you might feel like self-destructing; perhaps something has triggered this. The first step is to identify it. Once you have done this, you can work out what your core beliefs are (e.g. mine originally were not being good enough for anyone). In order to move forward, I had to practise self-compassion and be kind to myself. I also began to open up to people about how I was feeling and explained that my defences did occasionally need to go up.

TRAUMA BONDING

I don't know what your past relationships were like, or what your childhood was like, but trauma bonding is something that can have a huge impact on so many of us. If your needs aren't met as a child, you will do all you can to receive love and validation. Additionally, if you are going through trauma, you might bond over that shared trauma or you might find someone who you can get your esteem from, but in the long run this isn't going to help. I know this sounds brutal, but we need to get well for ourselves and find out who we really are. We need to heal from our past in order to move forward in a healthy way with relationships where we feel empowered to be who we are.

TELLING SOMEONE WHAT YOU HAVE BEEN THROUGH

It is important to work out when you are ready to tell a partner what you have been through. When I have been with people in the past, I've been very matter-of-fact. I say: "This is the deal. This is what I used to have." I expect them to not really fully understand.

You don't need to tell everyone you date that you have had an eating disorder, but if it is helpful for you to, then do it.

If a relationship is becoming more serious, then I would always recommend that you tell them. Honesty is so important and it will help you if in the future you have harder days. If they don't like it or don't take the time to understand it, then they aren't worth it.

Once I had done my matter-of-fact telling, I would often wait a few days and remind them they can ask me anything they want to about it and then work out with them how much detail they wanted to know. I always made it clear that I didn't want to be watched and I needed to be trusted, but I accepted that sometimes they would need to speak up if they were worried.

Work out what support you want and how your partner can really help you if you need it. Throughout it all remember they are not the enemy in this, despite what the eating disorder might tell you.

For me writing this all down always helped as a starting point and also gave them time to digest it before talking about it.

GETTING THE BALANCE RIGHT

I used to be a massive oversharer. I would tell people in the supermarket all about my week, stop and chat to someone on a train and tell them my life story; yes, you might think this is okay but oversharing is not always healthy. In fact, if we do it too much it is called "flooding". This is when you share so much with everyone that you begin to lose trust in yourself and your core foundation disappears. Again, something that I used to do a lot of, but it is important that you build foundations in your relationships before doing this.

Intimacy

We have talked already about body image (see Chapter 9), and, of course, how we feel about our looks is an important part of relationships. I know that I have struggled intimately, that sometimes I couldn't even be naked because I struggled with my body image. I am not going to sit here and tell you that when you meet someone who loves you all that goes away, because the reality is there is often more work to be done and it takes time. Don't beat yourself up about this. Again, it is about building up that support and trust.

Intimacy scared me for so long, combined with flashbacks to the abuse. For me, it was essential that I talked to my partner about this. Voicing it helped him feel included, and he realized that it wasn't about him or the sex as such, but about so much more.

Start slowly if that is helpful, have the lights turned off or dimmed, and gradually allow your partner to see more of you. Remember, they do love you for you and remember we all amplify those bits on our bodies we hate.

It is possible to have healthy relationships in recovery, but remember that communication is key.

EXERCISE 18: WARNING SIGNS

Take some time to think about the relationship you are in (this can work for friendships as well as intimate relationships). Think about those warning signs; the signs that your barriers might be going up and you might be pushing someone away, whether that is shutting yourself down from them, beginning to lie about food and exercise, or getting defensive about meal times. Can you first write those warning signs down? Next, write a letter to the person you are thinking about, explaining what you have been through, how they can help and what warning signs to look out for.

For example: *Dear X, I wanted to take the time to share something quite personal with you. I won't share everything just yet but if you have any questions, please do say. I want you to remember that it is me, I am still the same and you don't need to change how you act toward me. I had anorexia as a child and sometimes it still feels hard. Sometimes I can't be intimate because I am having a really bad body image day and my brain is being really nasty. On these days please be patient. When life gets harder, I am afraid things might creep back and, if they do, here are the signs to look out for...*

Top Tips

- Plan dates around *your* mealtimes and where you would like to eat – don't feel ashamed to do that. Choose something that works for you.
- Build your own self-worth. I was always expecting people to leave me and the reality is I have self-destructed a lot throughout relationships, never thinking I was worth being with.
- Take things slowly. Being intimate can feel difficult – go at the pace that feels right for you.
- Keep communicating and asking for support from your partner when you need it.

For Partners of Those with Eating Disorders

Dating someone with an eating disorder can be really challenging at times, while at the same time really sad. You have an amazing night out with drinks and a delicious meal… but hanging over you all evening is the worry about how your other half will feel the next day, having totally relaxed the night before. Or you fear that they will become distant as a way to cope with things.

If you are with someone who has an eating disorder, you may find the following insights helpful:

- Please remember none of this is about you!
- We aren't trying to control our eating or lose weight to please you; eating disorders aren't about trying to look good, but are about control, self-hatred, emotional numbing.
- We don't ever feel quite good enough to be with you or actually good for other things. We may never live up to the perfect ideal we think we should be.
- Control is key for us, which might mean that sometimes we get angry if plans around food change at the last minute.
- Even when we are in recovery it might take a while, if not years, to completely get rid of these tendencies.
- We may avoid sex or intimacy because we are ashamed of our bodies (if your partner has experienced sexual abuse, this may add another layer to this).

Things you can do to help:

- Don't be the food police.
- Don't comment on what your partner is eating.
- Don't plan surprises that involve food.
- Book self-catering holidays.
- Accept that your partner will have days when things might be harder and need extra time for themself.
- Educate yourself.
- Be patient.
- Take time out for yourself too.

BE AWARE OF UNRESOLVED ISSUES...
FROM DR OBUAYA

Sometimes difficulties in our relationships reflect internal struggles related to past trauma, which get "projected" to our partners. Past relationship difficulties, particularly abusive ones, can therefore unwittingly resurface. This is an unconscious process, e.g. you are not necessarily doing it deliberately. It does suggest that there are unresolved issues that need addressing.

Key Takeaway: You deserve to be loved, so start letting someone in because the right person will take time to understand you. I know this might feel super scary, but learn to trust yourself and then try and open yourself up to someone else.

CHAPTER 17

CLOTHES SHOPPING

When you have an eating disorder, clothes shopping is a real issue. I always struggled to find things that looked right. I remember when I was 12 years old, I was set on buying a specific coat. I went to get it on a Saturday morning, and when I wore it the following week someone commented on how it made me look really big. Right from then I hated it. What followed was years of trying to shop, getting in a state each time, not enjoying it, and giving up. I have now come to a place where I enjoy shopping and can find things I like and feel comfortable in, but it has taken time.

When I was in recovery, having to buy new clothes felt like the end of my eating disorder. I was saying goodbye to everything it had given me and in purchasing new clothes it was as if I was never going to go back there. Of course I didn't want to go back there, but it felt scary and hard making that decision. There was a period of time when I was doing this when I didn't want to get sick again, but was also afraid of being well.

There are three main reasons clothes shopping feels really hard in recovery:

1   Our bodies change shape.
2   A negative body image is often wrapped up in the illness.
3   Society telling us we have to be thinner.

These three things might feel hard to navigate, but they do get easier. We need to remember our bodies aren't supposed to stay the same size as they were when we were a child. Flooding our mind with more diverse body shapes will help us accept that everyone comes in different sizes and shapes.

EXERCISE 19: OUT WITH THE OLD!

The first step in revamping your wardrobe is to get rid of your old clothes; those that you link to your illness, those that perhaps you were competing to get into. Not only do we need to get rid of this competitive aspect, but we need to move into a place where we don't feel triggered by clothes. For example, if I had clothes that felt too tight, it would trigger my eating disorder thinking, and amplify my negative body image.

Hold a party or ceremony to get rid of all your old clothes. Get drinks in, have some nibbles, play music. Include your partner or others from your support network if that feels right to you.

However, although this is a fun exercise it is important to allow yourself to feel and grieve too as you get rid of the old. You may want to journal about how you're feeling afterwards.

Top Tips

MAKE A LIST

Make a list of some of the clothes you would like to buy.

Cover the basics, but also let yourself think outside the box. Try and channel some of your curiosity about recovery into trying new styles. I spent so long hiding my body, and at times I have to still check in with myself about this: am I only buying hoodies and jumpers or am I buying things I actually want to wear?

GO WITH SOMEONE YOU TRUST

Having someone to help and reassure you while shopping can be so helpful, but make sure it is someone you trust, someone who will be honest, and who you won't feel judged by.

FIND YOUR SIZE

A lot of people fall into the same trap when they are in recovery of buying clothes that hide their new shape. In the long run, this makes us feel worse mentally so it is important to challenge it. Remember that our brains will be distorting what we look like and how we feel.

Working out the correct sizes gets easier the more you go shopping, but remember that sizing can differ between shops. I tend to choose two sizes which allows me some variation in what I want to try on and helps me remember that sizes vary so much dependent on style. Once you have picked a selection of clothes, take a deep breath and head to the changing rooms. The lighting is never that great so just keep that in mind and remember that the eating disorder will probably be nagging away at you, making you feel so much worse.

When I was in recovery my mum took me to get properly measured for underwear at M&S. This helped me to work out what size I actually was so that my brain wouldn't be able to distort things quite as much. For some people it might be helpful to book in a proper fitting session. It might give you a clear idea about what you might want to wear, and what sort of clothes actually work.

TAKE YOUR TIME

Allow yourself time in the shops and in between so that you have some space to debrief with the person you are with. This will also allow you to check in with yourself and how you are feeling.

BE KIND TO YOURSELF

Be kind to yourself throughout and afterwards. Some days the shopping will get too much and on those days that is okay. Take your time, and if you are really struggling to find anything, stop shopping. Walk away from it – I have done this on numerous occasions and that is okay!

ONLINE CLOTHES SHOPPING

I know you'll have your own thoughts about online clothes shopping! Personally, I tend to steer clear from it. For some people though, it can make things easier. If you are someone who shops online, remember that sizes do vary so if you are able to, order a few sizes. When the clothes come, make sure you don't spend hours comparing yourself to the pictures on the internet. When we compare we always come off so much worse. Create a safe place to try things on at home, whether that is with others around or on your own, but limit the time you are trying things on.

KEEP ON TRYING... FROM DR OBUAYA

Concerns about your body are unlikely to shift dramatically overnight, so perseverance is key here. Adopting a mantra or positive self-talk may ease any anxiety associated with clothes shopping and help you start to develop a more positive body image.

Key Takeaway: Go clothes shopping with someone you trust and who you can be honest with about how you are feeling.

CHAPTER 18

FOOD SHOPPING

We all have to navigate the world of food shopping, but it can become more than just an everyday task to someone with an eating disorder. Normalizing this part of life is an important step in recovery, and in this chapter I'm going to show you some ways to do it so that it doesn't trigger huge amounts of anxiety or fear.

When I started out food shopping for myself after treatment, I would walk boldly into a shop, and then spend goodness knows how long pottering around, picking up everything, comparing everything, convincing myself that I wasn't really hungry and that I wasn't really in the mood for any of this. More often than not, I would leave with a mismatch of items – the lowest-calorie packs or the latest health crazes – feeling quite annoyed with myself. In my second year at university, when food shopping became a thing to do with housemates, I would do the same thing, but speed up my reading of labels, looking on amazed that no one else seemed to shop the way I did. I would return to our university house and make the most disgusting meal with whatever I had bought, thinking constantly about food and what I could have chosen instead.

Top Tips

PLAN YOUR SHOP
If you find grocery shopping hard, having a plan in place is key. By allowing yourself to plan ahead, it will help you to feel

less overwhelmed. Sit down beforehand and make a list of all the foods that you need. Think about the meals you might want to cook that week, then schedule an actual time to go. Once you're at the supermarket, don't rush, but don't linger! Never allow yourself to walk up and down an aisle more than twice, and limit aisle time to ten minutes max. Make sure you have time to yourself afterwards, especially if you find it very stressful.

DEALING WITH UNCERTAINTY

A lot of the anxiety comes from not being able to find the items on your list, or if the shop hasn't got a specific brand or portion size. This stuff gets easier to navigate with time, but at the start of your recovery have a back-up plan in place – for example, a second choice brand or a slightly different bread. Not being able to buy exactly what I wanted would have terrified me in the past, but over time it gradually felt more okay.

MOVE AWAY FROM SAFE FOODS

Everyone with an eating disorder has different safe foods, but if we stick to eating only these then our body will not fully recover and our condition will still have a hold over us. So over time when you are food shopping, I would encourage you to start to listen to your body more and think about what you might *want* to eat rather than what you perceive to be safe. One good approach is to make a list of safe and less safe foods, then each week add a less safe food to the shopping basket.

Try to vary what you buy. I know a lot of people eat similar foods each week and that is of course okay, but, for example, having two breakfast choices will help you to keep the eating disorder at bay. I would also challenge myself to pick something random like a packet of crisps or some chocolate.

IGNORE FOOD LABELS

This might feel like the most terrifying thing to do, and it takes time, but once we start to ignore the labels it helps us to move away from the eating disorder having any control over us. It might be extra hard for you if you've learned the labels of everything by heart anyway. If this is the case for you, then try to distract yourself when you are shopping. I normally find going with someone else or listening to a podcast helps to keep my mind elsewhere. If you have friends who read the labels religiously, then I would encourage you not to go food shopping with them!

KNOW YOUR TRIGGERS

Avoid the parts of the shop that you might find triggering, e.g. the diet sections or the signs saying sugar-free. I can be in these areas now and it doesn't impact me, but I know there was a time when it would have.

BREATHE!

You might walk into the store and be hit with full-blown anxiety. The last place you probably want to be is in a supermarket so stop, take a step back and breathe. Give yourself space to collect your thoughts and then try to carry on if you can, or contact someone for support if that helps.

HARDER TIMES OF THE YEAR

At certain times of the year, such as Christmas and Easter, food takes on even more significance and the supermarket aisles might be crammed with even more food and special offers, leading to an even greater feeling of being overwhelmed. Plan ahead to make sure you allow yourself enough time, and ideally go with someone else who can support you.

Online Food Shopping

Online food shopping can be really useful: you can limit the time you spend planning and doing your food shop much more easily than if you were walking around a shop. You can also create a list of "favourite" items which would be the stock food that you eat week to week. It does have its complications though: from the wrong stuff turning up (substitutions), or it may cause you to feel anxious as you scroll through pages of food. So be mindful of how online shopping is making you feel.

When I first was in recovery I used to get so annoyed when my choices were substituted for other items and often felt like I had to accept whatever came. But it is so important that you remember you don't have to. That you need to try and generate some confidence in pushing back and not feeling bad about it: if food comes and it isn't what you had asked for, you can send it back. Be bold in your decisions and thinking around this.

EXERCISE 20: PLANNING FOR A FOOD SHOP

1   Go through your cupboards and check what you already have (I always make sure I have some staples for cooking: olive oil, spices, pasta, etc.).

2   Think about your week ahead. What would you like to eat? What new foods might you be able to try?

3   Organize your list in the chart on the next page, bearing in mind the tip about safe and unsafe foods (see page 186).

What do I need in my cupboard?

Fridge foods

Vegetables and fruit

What am I going to try that is new?

IT WILL GET EASIER... FROM DR OBUAYA

Food shopping will probably be a daunting experience at first, but over time you will feel stronger and more confident to keep this going. Being proactive in facing your fears is a huge obstacle to overcome, one that will empower you and boost your self-confidence. It will get easier in due course.

Key Takeaway: PLAN, PLAN, PLAN!

CHAPTER 19

WEDDINGS

So you've got engaged and at first there's an amazing flood of excitement, followed closely by an overwhelming fear and anxiety ... There is so much stress around weddings that this rollercoaster of emotions can be true for most brides, but for someone with an eating disorder it becomes hugely magnified. From worrying about the food to finding a dress that fits... to worrying about having a "bad brain" on the actual wedding day... to feeling judged.

There is so much pressure to have the best day ever; for the wedding to be perfect, for us to look the best we have ever looked. All this can become so triggering, but the more we are aware and the more we plan, the less chance there is of our recovery being adversely affected.

BRIDEOREXIA

Eating disorders around weddings have become so common, there is now a name for them – "brideorexia", which affects one in ten brides. It is so sad that that is actually a thing, that we live in a world where we feel so pressured to look "perfect" on the day that we actually make ourselves ill. Wedding diets have become a whole industry. I recently went to a wedding fayre and of about 100 stands at least 30 of them were focused on weight loss – they even had a tent where apparently you could "massage yourself thin".

Dress Shopping

Shopping for the dress can feel like a really big deal and is anxiety-provoking. You might be unsure of who to take, afraid of being judged, or just worried about your body image. One thing to consider is that you don't *have* to wear a wedding dress – you can wear what you want. It is your day!

However, if you do decide you want a wedding dress, plan for the trip. I knew I would find it stressful with too many people, so I decided to take just my mum and sisters to the first few appointments while I got some courage to try on dresses. For my final appointment I took a close friend who I totally trusted and who I knew would be honest with me. I left that appointment with a dress I loved, as well as feeling confident in myself. Limiting the number of people you take to fittings will stop you getting too overwhelmed (remember, this goes for all dress shopping!).

- Try on different styles. Wedding dresses look totally different on, so make sure you see what is out there. I was lucky when I went to my fitting as I found a store, Brides Do Good, where the woman was so lovely and supportive and understood my body image feelings. I have heard stories of people who have been to try on a dress only to be told by the shop assistant they need to lose weight. We don't need to change who we are for the dress. The dress should fit us, not the other way around!
- Don't buy a dress that is too small for you – this is crucial because it will add unnecessary pressure on the day.
- Take photos at the fitting if you want to (and are allowed), but don't look at them afterwards. I wanted to share photos with family members and friends who hadn't been there, but don't look too hard and make sure you stop zooming in on the parts of yourself you might not like.
- Have a cuppa and a debrief with someone you trust afterwards. I made so many worry lists after I had been dress shopping! Keep talking and be honest with those around you.

- If it gets too much when you are shopping, walk away. I went to one appointment and my body image was so bad that day we gave up very quickly. It was frustrating, but also important to realize this was okay.

Food on the Day

Make sure you have the food you want. Whether it's a sit-down meal or buffet, work out what's best for you. This is something that you can be in total control of. Choose menus that work for you, and practise them beforehand so that you know what you are having. And make sure you sit yourself away from people who might comment on food portions and calories.

Timings on the Day

It can feel so easy to be sucked into what we "should" be doing, but in reality that doesn't matter! Look at what makes you and your partner happy and go for that instead. Book in some quiet time on the day for yourself to just stop and spend time with a select support group if you need to.

Pre-Wedding Diet Chat!

Feeling pressure to be the perfect size for a wedding is emotionally and physically exhausting, but each day we need to choose to recover. We need to choose to ignore those messages. For me this included not looking at other people's wedding photos on social media because I knew I might make comparisons. Instead of being sucked into this unhelpful dialogue and pressure, let's fight it! Because we will 100% enjoy the day more with our memories!

Top Tips

- Take some pressure off yourself and remember that you are there with those people who love you and want to be there for you.
- Have your support network in place. I knew at any point I could take my sisters or two close friends aside and say I am overwhelmed by the food and the day. They would be there if I had a panic. Sometimes having a code word might help. I also set up an SOS Wedding Day WhatsApp group so that I could message if I was having a wobble!
- Work out what you want to do about photos (definitely meet the photographer beforehand), and how you would feel if people share photos on social media on the day. I was fearful of this as I was worried I would look at my phone and see a photo of myself that might ruin my day. Being mindful of this is important.
- Position yourself away from anyone who might talk about calories or food.
- Focus on the memories and the fun, not the calories. This is easier said than done, perhaps, but have your coping mechanisms in place to stay in the moment. Make sure you have some distractions in place the day after in case you are worrying about the food you ate.

MANAGE YOUR EMOTIONS... FROM DR OBUAYA

We tend to apply the term "life event" to major losses in our life, such as bereavements, divorce and abuse. Although getting married is generally viewed as a positive life experience, it is still a life event and thus a potential source of stress. It is important to maintain strategies you may have picked up in managing stress and anxiety. If you ordinarily track your mood using a mood diary, this is an important time to keep an eye on it and consider how to deal with challenging periods.

Key Takeaway: Don't let societal pressure cause you to lose weight or do something you don't want to with your wedding day. Say yes to your wedding, but not to the eating disorder.

CHAPTER 20

HOLIDAYS AND TRAVELLING

When I was in hospital, I had lots of reasons for wanting to get well, both short- and long-term motivators, and a big one was travelling. I wanted to be able to experience the world and explore, but I never knew how this would be possible when I was living with such a fear of food. I was also convinced that I could travel when I was unwell – that I didn't need to get better first – but the fact is, if you go travelling or on holiday when you are unwell, you won't really enjoy it that much.

Again, as with other food routines, planning is important but the need for this will get less and less over time.

Dipping Your Feet into Travelling

Start with trips that are closer to home to give you the chance to experiment with a new routine. If you are starting out in recovery, or have only just left treatment, consider whether you feel ready for this step. Going away massively helped me, but at a point when I was able to eat snacks and meals with little guilt, and once I felt confident in working out what I needed to eat. Don't rush a trip if you aren't sure you are ready.

Working Out Where to Go

Be aware of your triggers. I struggled to be in swimwear in swimming pools, and at water parks or holiday parks, where everyone was in a more condensed space. I felt more comfortable at the beach. As I progressed through my recovery, while I still felt slightly body conscious at the beach, I gradually began to realize that bodies are different and we don't need to give into this pressure from society to have a "bikini body". As I travelled the world, I saw people of so many different shapes and sizes and I gradually began to reduce the pressure on myself.

When I was 18, my perfect holiday was laying on a beach, chatting and relaxing! I used to love being out in the sunshine, but over time this changed. When I began to work for myself, it changed again. I realized I struggled to switch off so having a holiday with activities was really helpful. Everyone is different, but for me having variety is key. Think about what your holidays might look like and do what is right for you. Don't risk your recovery by being somewhere you don't want to be where you are likely to be triggered.

Don't put yourself in a situation where you are on holiday with people who might adversely affect your recovery.

Holiday Food

Go self-catering, if possible, and on your first day, try to go to a supermarket. Buy some foods you know you feel comfortable eating. Remember, in some countries there might be slightly different brands, but just because it is a different brand doesn't mean it is bad for you or "unsafe". It helps to be in a country where you know you will like the food. For example, I love Middle Eastern and Asian food and know that when I holiday in those regions the food won't stress me out at all. Start trying different cuisines when you eat out. This will allow you to try different things and encourage you to be curious and work out the holiday destinations that will work for you in terms of eating.

Accountability While Away

Have someone that you feel accountable to – this doesn't need to be in person, but perhaps someone you can message to check in with and be honest with if you are struggling. This really does help. Having help with food was so important when I first used to travel. I remember when I went inter-railing after my first year at university and the only way to do it was by promising I would eat what my friend was eating. This worked until she decided to get something different to what we had agreed. I was so angry with her and upset about it, but it was at that point I had a decision to make. Either I let the anorexia come back and make me feel awful, or I pushed through. I chose to push through, and it was hard, but allowing myself this accomplishment also helped me to start to move further into a recovery space.

Top Tips

HAVE AN "EASIER" FOOD DAY IF NEEDED
I always allow myself (if I need it) one "easier" food day on holiday. This isn't a day of not eating or restricting, but about eating foods that perhaps I feel safer with.

SOCIAL MEDIA
Don't spend hours looking on social media comparing your holiday and "bikini" body to everyone else. I find body comparisons hard (and I always come off worse), so my way of dealing with it is to just not look. Also remember that social media doesn't show the complete story and the camera does lie!

TAKE "ME TIME"

Everyone needs time for themselves so take time out when you need it. Make sure you look after yourself and go at the speed that works for you.

DEALING WITH BAD DAYS

Some days might be harder, but on those days keep going. Distract yourself, talk to someone or write down your feelings, and then write off that day.

EXERCISE 21: REFLECT ON A RECENT TRIP

I always think it is helpful to reflect on the challenges we faced while we were away. This might be thinking about how you handled the different food options, or how you found the change of routine, or if you felt able to push your boundaries in recovery.

Take some time now to think about a recent trip, and how you responded to the return to your daily life.

To help with this, ask yourself:

1   What were your recovery wins on holiday?
2   How did you feel with the structure of the trip?
3   How did you manage the transition between home life and holiday?
4   What support did you have and how did it feel?
5   Were you honest with yourself and others?
6   Was there anything that would have helped?
7   Was there anything you had wished you had done (e.g. eaten a certain meal)?
8   How do you feel being back?

HOLIDAY PLANNING... FROM DR OBUAYA

Holidays may feel daunting because of the disruption in your routine and the uncertainty about how you will look after yourself in an unfamiliar environment. Remember that it's normal to feel a degree of anxiety. Before you travel, do spend some time putting together a contingency plan, which should outline key contacts you can reach out to for support if needed.

Key Takeaway: Think about what your holiday would be like if you were in a good space in recovery – dream big! What would it be like to not be body conscious? Now set yourself a goal to go on that holiday!

CHAPTER 21

DEALING WITH CHALLENGING LIFE EVENTS

People often say that the most stressful life events are bereavement, divorce, getting married and moving house (and maybe also a pandemic?). So what do you do when this happens? What do you do when you want to switch off all these feelings and emotions, and to feel in control again?

Life can feel so unpredictable at times, from losing a loved one, to facing trauma or dealing with new life circumstances like becoming a parent. A lot of what we have discussed in the book will hopefully help you when facing these things, and the skills you develop along the way will help you to move forward. In recovery, it is important to realize that we pick up new behaviours along the way, that our coping mechanisms change, and if we embed these firmly, they will help us stay in a positive mindset.

Treatment varies so much across the country and while some of us might have had amazing treatment others might have found it a bit harder. I feel that I have set myself some really firm foundations in my recovery and rearranged some of my coping mechanisms in a more positive way. Have a think about your foundations of recovery. Are they firmly set in stone? Are you confident that you have what it takes to deal with what life throws at you?

CASE STUDY: KATHY

Our three children were conceived with the help of prayer and drugs to help ovulation. This is where the eating disorder story really started. I lost weight after each birth and gradually my weight and health declined. This was all combined with what I now know to be a controlling marriage relationship, which ultimately turned abusive. It wasn't until my youngest was nine months old that I was diagnosed with anorexia, resulting in my first admission (no day treatment back then). I was devastated to be separated from my children who were looked after by friends in the daytime, the church people helping my husband out with meals, etc. I am still so grateful for the kindness of people who nurtured my kids. I could never shake the guilt I felt during those admissions. However, the main reason I chose to write about my experience is to encourage any prospective mums-to-be who are presently battling eating disorders. Let your longing for a baby really spark motivation for self-care. This is the best example of loving yourself in order to love another I can think of. Unless you push past the obsession to keep weight just under what is your unique "set point", my experience bears out, your fertility could well be affected. When you do find out you are pregnant, you more than likely will experience pregnancy nausea, hopefully not actual sickness, but believe me, if you have not learned to feed yourself well, eating through nausea may prove to be the challenge that takes you by surprise. The best way through it is to eat continually, don't allow your stomach to be empty. Yes, you heard right!! I actually loved my changing shape; I was so overjoyed that I welcomed all pregnancy changes.

PREGNANCY AND RECOVERY

I spoke to a few people who had been through pregnancy and gathered their tips for you:

- First things first, if you are thinking of having a baby or are pregnant, it is really important to tell your midwife about your history with an eating disorder. Make a list of all the things worrying you from weight change, to hunger changes and take these with you. I know this might feel hard to do but the sooner we start this conversation the better.
- Be mindful of old trauma resurfacing – schedule some appointments with your therapist if you have one and if you don't, try journalling to help you process your emotions.
- Allow yourself to feel things! Your emotions might be a bit all over the place during pregnancy and beyond – and that is okay! It is so important that we are kind to ourselves and at the same time mindful that the eating disorder might use this as a chance to suck us back in to offer us that sense of control. If you feel this happening, try and speak up!
- A lot of people think that because someone is pregnant it gives them even more right to comment on a person's weight. Please be mindful of this and establish ground rules in your own pregnancy. Perhaps take some time to work these out at the start of your pregnancy, and then if someone does overstep the mark, have your sentence in your head to respond (for example, "My weight is off limits").
- Remember that not all baby bumps look like they do in magazines!

- Be aware of how your body will change, not just appearance but hunger and digestion-wise.
- Invest in practical clothes, but also items that make you feel good about yourself!
- Remember how amazing your body is for doing what it is doing. I know this might not always seem easy but distract yourself with planning for the birth, with creating keepsakes, and focusing on other things.
- Stay alert even when the baby is born; post-partum bodies can feel difficult at times and so be kind to yourself. Be mindful of what you look at on social media.
- If you need practical support after the baby is born with meals being cooked for you, don't feel afraid to ask.
- Keep being honest with those around you. I know this can feel challenging at times, especially when the eating disorder might be telling you to be secretive, but it is important that you have people that you can feel accountable to. Going through pregnancy can feel really challenging at times and so it is important to make sure you don't feel alone in this time.

Dealing with Emotions

When something happens in life, we respond emotionally. Whether it is grieving over a loved one, or feeling nervous about exams, or being stressed about moving house. These feelings are okay and we need to find a way to acknowledge them and sit with them. In the past you will have used food to manage these feelings, but in recovery you need to find new coping mechanisms. If you are feeling emotions you don't want to feel, or you want to control, take some time to understand them. I found talking, journalling, and getting out in the sunshine all good coping mechanisms.

What is most important is not to shut off your feelings. Start by acknowledging and naming your emotions. Allow yourself to think about what has caused you to feel this way and begin to process it. This bit might feel really hard and uncomfortable, but it will allow you to move forward.

Take as much time as you need to sit and be with those emotions, writing things down if you need to or perhaps you're someone who prefers to draw or paint. Do whatever works for you. We don't know how long these things take to pass and for each of us it might be different. Work through the pain, and the wound.

Be aware of your triggers. Perhaps a relationship has ended and you are mourning it, but every time you go on social media, you look at your ex-partner's profile. If this is the case, block it, unfriend them. Do what it takes to stop that wound opening back up.

Negative People

We need to be aware of people in our lives who might be gaslighting us or manipulating us in other ways. Sometimes just realizing that these people won't hear us and aren't good for us is an important step to moving forward. Please be mindful of this and if you find yourself ruminating over it, invest in some time for yourself and go back to those distractions that you have established.

Top Tips

TALK ABOUT IT
Find a way to express yourself in a way that you feel heard that doesn't involve food or exercise. Share with someone where you are at; seek that support professionally or with friends. Allow yourself space to talk it through, to hash it out. By doing this

vocally it will help to stop ruminating at night. Just to flag here, I am a real advocate for talking about things, but I think over time, we need to stop going over things if we are doing it in a way that is causing an increase in rumination and having a negative impact on ourselves. It always helped me to write something down and then try to voice it.

DON'T BOX UP YOUR FEELINGS

So often in life we hide the trauma, and we tick along pretending things are okay. When challenging things happen in life, we need to acknowledge them, give ourselves space to process our feelings, and be kind to ourselves.

FIND ANOTHER WAY TO PROCESS WHAT IS HAPPENING

Using trial and error is key here; work out the best ways for you to process things, work out how you feel about things and what works for you. Sometimes distraction is important, but you also need to allow yourself to acknowledge and heal.

BE PATIENT WITH YOURSELF

Give yourself time and space to deal with whatever you're coping with.

EXERCISE 22: WHAT WORKS FOR YOU?

Take some time to make a list of healthy coping mechanisms. Think about what you like doing; think about what makes you happy and gives you the space to process things.

Think about what you have found helpful over the last few months and at times in your recovery. It might also be worth looking at what others do on social media.

For me a few that would feature are:

1   Talking to my partner, sister or best friend – identify these individuals. Well worth having a few to go to just in case one isn't around.

2   Booking a trip with X – travel is a big thing for me that helps me stay well but it could be anything from booking a holiday, to a day out or a walk with someone.

3   Reading – find a good book and get stuck into it.

Let's Recalibrate

As we come to the end of Part 3, I wanted to check in with you. You might not be feeling any differently from when you started this book; you might be frustrated that you got a copy of this hoping for a quick fix. I wanted to end with six tips for any time of life – these are things that I think we need to be doing weekly.

TIP 1: SELF-CARE, AND LOTS OF IT!

I am excellent at telling people to take days out for self-care activities, but the reality is I am terrible at doing this for myself. I spend far too much time focusing on other things in my life. At the moment I am trying to do one self-care activity every week, such as having a coffee in one of my favourite cafés, getting my nails done, watching a girly movie. There are so many amazing ideas online if you need inspiration. Self-care doesn't have to be expensive – just things we do for ourselves. And YES you do deserve to do this!

TIP 2: KNOW YOUR MOTIVATIONS

When I was in hospital and in the depth of my anorexia, I had my motivations to get well written down on prompt cards. I would carry them in my pocket and if things got tough, I would pull them out to remind myself. It meant I didn't have to think when I was having a bad day and it helped me keep on track when life seemed so tough. While I now don't need to carry these cards, I have them in my recovery box under my bed just in case. Take some time today to make a list of why you want to get well or stay fighting and use these as prompts when you need them.

TIP 3: DON'T LET THE BAD DAYS WIN

Don't let one bad day throw you. I have days when I don't get up and days when I try on my entire wardrobe feeling completely trapped. But I now know that if you have a bad day, the best thing to do is let it finish and then write it off. The next morning, however hard it is to wake up, start afresh and give it a go again. Recovery isn't a straight line and can be hard work, but it is definitely achievable. It's well worth fighting to get to a point where you can manage it.

TIP 4: BE BUILT UP BY PEOPLE AROUND YOU

Have people around you who build you up and make you feel good. This is a tricky one, but you need those people. You need people who you trust and who understand you, or at least try to. You need people who don't get fed up with you if you're going through a bad patch and who will take the time to learn how to respond to your needs. We also need to work out who is in our support network. Some people are there to support us, some of our friends are there for fun, and some are there for distractions. Who is in your network? Are they good for your mental health? Are they building you up? Are they on your team or are they knocking you down?

TIP 5: KEEP TALKING

Talk. Probably the most important of all my tips, and one that I do struggle with from time to time. When I first left hospital I had become excellent at sharing how I felt. However, nine years later after my grandma passed away, I didn't feel able to express myself. I hated feeling all this emotion, so I shut myself off from those around me and resorted to my old ways of living. After nearly ending my life by suicide, I knew I had a choice to make: either I gave up or I talked about how I felt and I fought back. And so I talked. This relapse taught me that no, I wasn't weak, but I must keep talking. Opening up is scary but it really helps!

TIP 6: REMEMBER

Our bodies aren't supposed to stay the same shape and will change as we get older!

EXERCISE 23: THREE THINGS

Write three things that you are going to do daily that you have learned and three things you will do weekly. For example:

Daily: Naming something I am thankful for.

Weekly: Checking in with myself about how I feel – and telling someone.

Daily

1

2

3

Weekly

1

2

3

Make a commitment to yourself now to make a choice to recover. Choosing recovery may feel hard and scary, but it is so worth it.

BUILDING RESILIENCE... FROM DR OBUAYA

Resilience has become a buzzword in mental health, but is a key concept as it recognizes that progress and growth are not always linear. Life inevitably throws up challenges and setbacks, some predictable, others less so; that need not be the end of your story. Aiming for a stress-free life may sound appealing but is unrealistic. Resilience is the ability to achieve your full potential and to continue to develop in the face of adversity.

Developing a structure to help you navigate daily life using some of the tools outlined in this book, adopting a growth mindset and surrounding yourself with people that provide a positive influence are key pillars to becoming more resilient.

Key Takeaway: Recovery can be so hard at times but it is possible! Set yourself small goals, keep focused on the end game and surround yourself with people who will build you up and help you!

PART 4
MANAGING RELAPSE

CHAPTER 22

ABOUT RELAPSE

Relapse – that dreaded word. The possibility of it happening might often be at the forefront of your mind, filling you with fear if you have just left treatment. Or perhaps you are in the midst of a relapse right now and feel like you are heading right back to "that place" again, with no idea how to stop it. Hang in there. If you haven't relapsed, or don't feel you will relapse, that's great but it *doesn't* mean the eating disorder is less serious. Recovery is not always linear and while that is frustrating and annoying, it is important to remember this.

This chapter will walk you through the different stages of a relapse you may encounter and the reasons why relapses can happen.

Stages of Relapse

To become aware of a potential relapse, we need to understand the process and spot the signs that we are spiralling. Terence Gorski is an American psychologist who through his work has identified three stages of relapse: an emotional relapse, then a mental relapse, and then a physical relapse.[10]

---

10 Gorski, T (1990). The Cenaps Model of Relapse Prevention: Basic Principles and Procedures. *Journal of Psychoactive Drugs*, 22(2), pp. 125–133.

EMOTIONAL RELAPSE

How is your general emotional state? Are you feeling anxious? Are you feeling sad? And how long have you felt this way? It is at this stage that we need to tune in and then step up and practise some self-care – whether that's journalling, pampering, taking time out – whatever it is that works for you. I normally email someone close to me and tell them I have been struggling and that I feel quite stuck and unhappy. I find that the simple act of telling someone at this early stage really helps. It allows me to start to move forward. It also gives someone the chance to help me manage my emotions and give me clarity. For example, during the COVID-19 lockdown I emailed my older sister to flag my mood to her. She responded by suggesting that we message something positive to each other each day. Sounds simple, doesn't it? But it does help!

MENTAL RELAPSE

This is when the unhealthy coping mechanisms start to flood your mind. Part of your brain wants to fight them, but the other part is being tempted back. You might start to plan your relapse and imagine how it could work. You might begin to let the eating disorder dictate your day and think of ways to get out of future meals out with friends or family. At this point it is important to tell someone what is going on. If you don't, the eating disorder will use this as a chance to try and pull you in deeper and deeper. At this point, you are feeling slightly guilty for eating or not exercising enough but you still feel a little in control.

PHYSICAL RELAPSE

This is when you actually start to take the voice of the eating disorder seriously. You start to allow it to pull you back in with its false promises and false reassurances. This is the hardest stage to come back from. It is possible, but I want to help you prevent your relapse escalating to this point in the first place.

CASE STUDY: CARA

I was first diagnosed with anorexia as a young teenager around 17 years ago and admitted to a psychiatric hospital for six months, which helped me to manage both my eating and my low mood. Once I was discharged, I relapsed quite quickly but was able to manage my symptoms. Although I eventually reached a stage of being semi-recovered – I was maintaining a healthy weight – the anorexic thoughts hadn't gone away.

When I turned 18, I was discharged from CAMHs, and it wasn't until my early twenties that I had another severe relapse, which resulted in me being treated by the adult community eating disorders service. This treatment was ineffective and I didn't make any progress, so a few months later I ended up having another course of therapy with them. After being well for a number of years, I relapsed again last year and this time I was too unwell for therapy, so spent almost seven months in a day patient programme, which is a middle ground between outpatient and inpatient. I am now receiving another course of therapy and I hope this will be my last time under the service.

My advice to anyone going through this is to talk to somebody. Eating disorders thrive on secrecy, and I know that reaching out for help and support has been the first step for me in getting better. Being honest about my thoughts, feelings and behaviours has given me the best chance of recovery. I also think it's really important to be honest with yourself. Don't let anorexia trick you into thinking you can lose just a small amount of weight and be happy, or that you will only use a certain behaviour just this once. Anorexia is sneaky and it will take any window of opportunity that it is given to sink its teeth back in; it's important to be aware and to catch these thoughts early.

Relapse can lead to lots of feelings of shame and guilt, but something that has really helped me is reminding myself that it's not my fault. My therapist recently said to me, "It's not your fault that you have anorexia, but it is your responsibility to make the right decisions that contribute to your recovery." I don't see recovery as one big choice, but as a series of small decisions that need to be made over and over again. It's not an absence of difficult thoughts, but having the skills and resources to manage those thoughts and be able to challenge them as they arise.

Recovery is not a straight line and for some, relapse does happen. Please don't let shame or fear stop you from reaching out and admitting you need support again; it's nothing to be ashamed of. You deserve to be free from anorexia.

Why Relapse Can Happen

Relapsing may feel like the best option; it might feel like your *only* option. Your eating disorder might be your way of showing people you are not okay. What's important is to find another way to communicate this – by talking, by journalling, in whatever way works for you. I get how hard that can be and how hard that feels, but if we challenge ourselves to do it then it will make us stronger by the end.

Resorting back to eating disorder behaviours can make you feel better in the short term, but it won't in the long term. You might tell yourself, like I did, that you'll do this for a bit, feel better, and then stop again. But eating disorders aren't as straightforward as that. Take stock and think about how far you have come. Think about all the positives of recovery from going out with your friends, to having energy to do something, to creating memories. By moving the focus on to those things it will help firstly bring back some happy memories, and secondly remind you that there is more to life than weight. I make it sound easy, don't I? And trust me, I know it isn't, but it is possible to get back into that better recovery space.

Feeling Shame

There are so many emotions when it comes to relapse – the excitement of entering into that relationship with the eating disorder, the frustration and anger that it is happening, the feelings of shame and weakness when we start to realize what might be going on. In my relapse I felt shame, unworthiness, loneliness… You may have felt these too, but remember that relapses don't mean you are weak. Shame is dangerous because it may prevent you from seeking help – don't let it. Work out who you can honestly speak to about your feelings. Who you can be really vulnerable with. We need these people in our recovery and I would encourage you to take some time to think about who is there for you.

SEEKING HELP

I know I talk a lot about the importance of getting the right support around you. If you are reading this feeling like you have nowhere to go, that is okay. If you don't have a direct support group, please do seek help elsewhere. Have a look at the online support forums, helplines and groups in the Resources section on page 239. I really encourage you to find what works for you. You might find it helpful to connect with like-minded people on social media – for me, it really helps to follow and hear regularly from others who have experienced similar things and who have come through it.

My Relapse Story

When I relapsed in 2016, I was so frustrated – there is no hiding that. I was angry at myself and those people around me. Angry and embarrassed that I had spent a year in treatment, but for some reason couldn't keep going. I felt myself being pulled backwards.

It all began at the start of the year. After a lovely three-week holiday in Sri Lanka, I had settled into working life again, but was conscious that my grandma was very ill. She had dementia and was getting worse weekly. Living in Abingdon made it hard to see her, but I tried to visit every few weeks.

I remember the penultimate time I saw my grandma as vividly as if it was yesterday. We lay in her bed in her wonderful house. I had always loved being at her house – sitting in her garden, baking in the conservatory, reading her poetry by TS Eliot. She loved listening to it and always pointed out when I deliberately missed bits to get to the end quicker! That day I was there with her for hours, reading and talking; her cat Lilly, stretched out on the end of the bed...

Just a fortnight later she went into a care home. I visited her with my mum and I hated it. I didn't like seeing her in there. She looked so different from just two weeks before and I was so confused. I couldn't even hide the relief when it was time to go. I headed to her house to help pack some bits. It felt so empty without her there. As I stood in the kitchen, I thought back to all the wonderful summers I'd had there. I held it together so well in front of my mum, but once I was on the train alone, the tears began to stream down my face. The guilt set in – I was annoyed that I hadn't been able to handle the care home. I kept going over and over it in my head, trying to work out what I could have done better, what I should have said, how I should have looked at her. It was ruining me. By the time I got on the tube that evening, I told myself it would be fine. I would visit the week after. I could talk to her then, read to her, do what she wanted... it would be fine.

But it wasn't...

There was no next time.

The following Tuesday my mum phoned and told me it wasn't looking good. I was terrified, I wanted to be strong. I knew I had to be. I didn't want anyone to see me struggling. I went for a run. I told myself it would be okay if I ran faster and if I ran over all the double drains (back then, that was a superstition). I pushed myself that morning in a way I hadn't done for ages. I told myself keep running, faster, faster and she won't die; she will fight on. I believed I could control that if I did this properly.

But it didn't work. I got a call at work about an hour later, and had to leave immediately. By the time we arrived at the care home, it was too late. I never got to say sorry to my grandma. I never even got to say goodbye.

After my grandma passed away, I was really struggling to deal with my emotions. I blamed myself for her death. I beat myself up because I hadn't been able to support her the way I should have. Everything I did to suppress these feelings didn't seem to be working – the long hours in the office, putting on a brave face … I was frustrated and longing to feel okay again. The anorexia started slowly but surely to come back; it sucked me in, giving me false promises, giving me a false value and making me feel better.

And the truth is I loved having it back in my life at that moment, as the hole inside me began to shrink. Eating disorders do that. They pull us back in, make us feel better emotionally, and it works at first, but then the guilt sets in and we realize how destructive it is. Before we know it we are back in that battleground, facing those mines, as our brain tells us we are a failure if we eat, but weak if we give in and let the eating disorder take control.

After a few months of struggling I knew I had to act. I was desperate to not get sick again, but didn't know how to manage alone. With my mum's support and some tough love, I went to my doctor and got a referral for an appointment with the eating disorder service…

I couldn't believe I was sitting in a mental health hospital after so long. The anorexia was screaming at me that I was a failure for reaching out for support, grilling me on what I was doing sitting in that seat. It was such a different experience to when I was younger. I was now sitting there not in denial, but knowing I wanted help. I even went for a wee when I arrived to make sure I was going to be as light as possible when they weighed me. I felt quite agitated and tried so hard to shut off that voice in my head.

"Jennifer Hope Virgo". My name pierced through the waiting room. I looked up at the woman standing there. Mum squeezed my hand and said, "Let's do this," and we headed into the room together. I talked so openly about everything. I had worked out what I wanted and what support I thought would be best for me. We talked about how I had been feeling and I was so honest (despite the anorexia guilt-tripping everything I did).

After an hour or so of being there, the clinician said, "I am sorry, but your BMI just isn't low enough."

I laughed and said, "I knew that would be the case." (See page 51 for what to do if this happens to you.)

She said she would send a letter to my doctor outlining a few other options, such as medication and a referral for CBT (a 12-week wait at least!), but I had switched off. I was trying to contain myself, but my brain was screaming again. Getting louder and louder. The next four weeks turned into a cycle of crying, exercising and feeling suicidal. I felt trapped and so alone with it all. I hated what was happening, I hated how my brain was responding to this and how it was making me feel, but could see no way out of it. I was back in that battleground and the more I pushed away the anorexia, the more it shouted at me, the more of a fight it put up.

After nearly ending my life, I ended up going back to my doctor. I made sure I saw a doctor that understood my condition. I went on medication and agreed to have check-ins over the next few months. Before I went on medication, I was terrified of it. I was afraid of putting on weight, afraid of losing motivation, afraid of the side effects. I basically catastrophized the whole thing! After this initial fear I realized that I just needed to start. And after a few days I ended up taking the tablets. There were a few side effects, mainly headaches, lack of sleep and bad dreams, but after a few weeks things felt a bit easier. It cleared my head, gave me energy and helped me to feel able to push forward in my recovery. Not everyone needs to go on medication, but it was a path I chose. I told myself I would be off it in six months max, but this pressure made it harder, and instead I ended up being on it for the next four years. Going on medication isn't a weakness. It may not be for you, but think about what's stopping you taking it. Bear in mind that if you had a physical illness, you wouldn't hesitate to treat it, so why should it be different for a mental illness?

Check Your Foundations

Because of the treatment I had the first time, I was very lucky that I had strong foundations to build on. If you fear relapsing or are in the middle of a relapse, look at what foundations you have in place and don't be afraid to use them.

Relapsing can make you feel weak and like a total failure. The frustration you feel toward yourself and those around you will get deeper and deeper. Eating disorders are also extremely competitive illnesses, so when you get turned away from support services you feel like even more of a failure.

Remember:

1 Relapsing does not make you weak.
2 It gives you the chance to come back even stronger.

IN DENIAL?

I know for a lot of us we might see fitness crazes on social media and think it's okay for us to join in, or we might justify our eating because someone else has disordered eating, but the fact is whatever the disordered eating or new fitness craze, it is NOT okay! I know how easy it is for me to sit here and write this but sometimes when we see it plastered everywhere it can feel really hard to believe. But please remember this as you go forward into the next section, and be open-minded about your plan of action.

WHY ADDRESSING RELAPSE IS IMPORTANT... FROM DR OBUAYA

Research into eating disorders suggests that one in two people who developed eating disorders in their teenage years achieve long-term recovery, i.e. being healthy and functioning well psychologically. Another one in five experience a reduction in their symptoms. The best chance of recovery was when treatment was started in the first three years of the onset of the symptoms.[11] This emphasizes the need to seek professional help and remain in contact with those professionals as much as possible. Relapse may feel like a backward step, but support should be sought as soon as possible to improve the likelihood of long-term recovery.

---

11 Steinhausen *et al* (2003). The outcome of adolescent eating disorders: findings from an international collaborative study. *European Child & Adolescent Psychiatry*, 12, pp. 91–98.

CHAPTER 23

TAKING ACTION

So what next? You have relapsed or feel yourself slipping. What can you do?

Firstly, don't wait until things get worse. What is most important is that you have realized that you are relapsing and to make a plan straight away and get help.

Step 1: Call Your Doctor Now

Get yourself an appointment with your doctor straight away. If you have a doctor already that doesn't really "get" the eating disorder, find another one. Whatever your size or shape, if you are struggling, you need professional support.

Step 2: Write Meal Plans

These can provide structure and routine. I wrote meal plans and had a weekly grocery shop booked, always making sure that I had a sit-down meal in the evening with someone. As you get further into your recovery, you can gradually rely less on meal plans, but they are useful in the early stages.

Step 3: Work Out Your Support Network

Who do you have in your corner and what are their roles? I had my mum and sister there to check in on me, my boyfriend to remind me why I needed to stay well, friends to distract me and have fun with. Sometimes being vulnerable around people can be hard, especially when we are relapsing. But the more we let people in, even though it may feel really uncomfortable, the easier it will be and the better it is for our recovery.

Step 4: Be Accountable to Someone

This is someone that you can be really honest with and someone that will be honest with you. My partner and sister were both straight-talking about meals and exercise. It was frustrating at times, but in the long term it really helped.

Step 5: Journal!

This was essential for me in helping process my feelings – in recovery and through my relapse. If writing long reams about yourself isn't for you, try a bullet journal which encourages doodling and being creative on the page, as a way of getting your emotions across.

Step 6: Distract Yourself

When your brain won't stop with unhelpful thoughts, it is important to train yourself to think about something else. Actively turning your attention to something else entirely will help you to stop ruminating. Identify times in the day when you are more likely to ruminate; for me, it was mainly in the evenings and when I was lying in bed. Try watching TV, doodling, painting your nails, calling a friend or going for a walk.

IDEAS FOR A BAD DAY

1   Get out of bed even on days that you don't want to.
2   Wash your hair.
3   Leave the house for at least 30 minutes (this doesn't include going to the gym or for a run).
4   Go to a café.
5   Go home and put on your pjs and loungers.
6   Keep caring for others and be there to offer support even when you are in need too.
7   Send a note, card or flowers to someone who you appreciate.
8   Talk to someone.
9   Journal.
10   Write three things you are looking forward to.
11   Write three things you are grateful for.
12   Write three good things from the last week.
13   Allow yourself to cry.
14   Nap if you need to.
15   Remember that you are not alone.
16   Walk away from the mirror if your brain is being nasty.
17   Practise self-care and relax before bedtime.
18   Remind yourself that this feeling will pass and tomorrow is another day.

Step 7: Book Some Fun Activities

Think about those things you like doing – travelling, going out with friends, perhaps. Whatever it might be, get booking! Start creating happy memories again and it will help you remember that there is more to life than the eating disorder.

Step 8: Make Lists

Planning will help you stay focused on your goals, and motivate you to stay well. Update your list periodically because your motivations and goals will change.

EXERCISE 24: WHAT'S YOUR PLAN?

It can help to write your plan down to stay focused. Use this chart to add as much detail as possible about what might work for you. I've put some examples at the start.

STEP	ACTION
Make the doctor aware that you are struggling	*Book a doctor's appointment. Write out what I want to say.*
Distraction from rumination	*Painting my nails, watching a new box set*

STEP	ACTION

Barriers to Seeking Help

Take some time to think about why you find it hard to be vulnerable. Perhaps you have been hurt in the past. Perhaps you always come across as the strong person, so don't want to appear weak. Or perhaps you are worried about being judged. It can be tough to push through these barriers and reach out, but it is so important to do so.

ADVICE FOR PARENTS OR CARERS IN RELAPSE... FROM DR OBUAYA

Do try to support your loved one in developing a crisis plan *before* you find yourself in a crisis situation!

As frustrated as you may feel by the situation, it is best to try to adopt a gentle, inquisitive and caring approach, avoiding confrontation and any judgement or blame. Where possible, avoid focusing solely on their food or weight.

Try to avoid raising any concerns you may have either side of mealtimes, as this can be a particularly stressful time for your loved one.

Try not to respond to or be upset if the initial response to your concern is anger or denial. This is common and is usually a defence mechanism, i.e. your loved one is not necessarily angry at you, but rather the situation they find themselves in, which can be extremely anxiety-provoking.

Try to show consistent warmth and concern. It will help your loved one to feel held.

Do seek support for yourself if you feel that the situation is having an adverse impact on your own mental health. You may benefit from speaking to other carers in similar positions to you through formal support groups, or require support from your doctor or a mental health specialist.

EXERCISE 25: FACT-PLANNING FOR YOUR DOCTOR'S APPOINTMENT

Before you go to your doctor's appointment (go as soon as you feel you are relapsing), I would suggest completing these sentences (adapt them if you need to):

I struggled with [Insert eating disorder] in the past.

The treatment I had before was [insert treatment].

Over the last [insert time-frame] I have been feeling [emotion] and noticed behaviours starting to come in. I think about food [X amount] a day.

The behaviours that are coming back are [insert behaviours] which makes me feel [insert emotion].

I really do not want to slip any further, but I need some help.

In an ideal world we would immediately be offered support! But the reality is, we don't live in a world like that. If you reach out for support when you relapse and you aren't able to get it, please know that this is not your fault. You do deserve that support, but you might need some interim support in place. Always ask for this when you go to the doctor. Be direct, and bold!

Whether you have relapsed once or multiple times, it is important to remember that with the right support you can get back on top of it again. With the right treatment, and support network and coping mechanisms, I know you can do this!

EXERCISE 26: WRITE A RELAPSE PREVENTION PLAN

The purpose of this plan is to have all those red flags in place, to be self-aware, and to make others aware. Once you have written this, I suggest finding someone to go through it with you. This means you are both in the same place when it comes to managing things.

Please remember that this will be unique to you and you can alter what you put in it, but what I would suggest is:

1 **Identify likely triggers:** e.g. grief, change in living arrangements, loss of a loved one, relationship ending.
2 **Identify external unhealthy behaviours** (those that others can see): e.g. over-exercising, changing food patterns, looking distracted at mealtimes, missing events.
3 **Identify internal unhealthy behaviours** (ones that you know about, but others will only know if you tell them): e.g. calorie-counting, how you feel in yourself.

Remember...

- Don't beat yourself up if you relapse. Relapse is not a sign of weakness, but you need to find the strength to push yourself through it.
- Don't feel ashamed or guilty.
- Get help: there are so many organizations out there and you deserve support.
- Talk!

CRISIS PLANNING... FROM DR OBUAYA

It is hard to problem solve in the middle of a crisis, so crisis planning is best done in advance.

Find a friend or loved one who can work through the plan with you.

A crisis plan should include the names and contact details of the health care professionals/services you would reach out to in an emergency, including "out-of-hours", i.e. evenings, weekends and bank holidays!

CONCLUSION

One thing you will have learned from your own experience and from reading this book is that recovering from an eating disorder is really, really tough! There will be good days and bad days and a big part of successful recovery is about learning how to manage the difficult times. Even when you are in full recovery, you may still have challenging days. It is so important that you know your triggers, can spot the signs, and that you ask for help. Most importantly, don't panic – you aren't necessarily getting unwell again.

Twelve years ago I was living in a hospital with super-strict menus and mealtimes; I am proud of how far I have come. I never thought I would be able to live outside of treatment, let alone live on my own. Yes, I still have the odd bad day, but I am in a space where I can get through these, where I have firm foundations that stop me getting unwell again. I now know that on the bad days it doesn't mean I am relapsing and it doesn't make me weak. I can push ahead despite those feelings.

What I can also guarantee you is that living life in recovery and without the eating disorder is so much better than letting it win. If you are reading this and you don't fully believe me, hold on to all those reasons to get well and to stay well. Push those boundaries and soon you will experience the joy of eating out, the laughter that comes with last-minute plans. The energy you now have to think about other things.

I know recovery is really hard at times but it can be so good too.

EXERCISE 27: WHERE ARE YOU AT NOW?

This exercise was at the very start of the book on page 40. I now invite you to use the same questions to reflect on how far you've come. What areas do you still need to work on? What are your triggers? Use what you discover here to go back to the earlier exercises if you need to. I would encourage you to return to this exercise again and again and reflect on what you've achieved and what you still need to do to stay in recovery.

1   What does recovery mean to you?

2   Where do you feel you are at?

3   Where do you want to be?

To help you answer these questions, ask yourself:

- How often do I think about food?
- Does food stop me going out?
- Do I limit social interactions because I am worried about food?
- Do I think about exercise all the time?

4   How has your journey changed over the last few years? Think back to where your recovery started – how do things compare? What are some positives and things you learned?

MY REASONS TO STAY WELL

Not thinking about calories all the time
Last-minute meals out – Travelling the world
Headspace to think about other things
Late-night glasses of wine – Not setting
alarms for gym sessions – To have more energy
To campaign – To have my own family
To eat pancakes – To eat jam on toast – To
run marathons – So my life isn't dictated by
food times – To keep cycling around the world
So I don't have to eat Frusili bars unless I want
one – So I can keep working – So I can focus on
other things and not just food – So my hair keeps
growing – For the laughter – So that I don't
always have to have a plan in place for food
when I go out – So I don't feel like crying all the
time – So my brain stops beating me up – So I
start to feel happy with my body – To fulfil my
dreams – So I can be engaged at mealtimes and
not stressing about food – So I don't miss out on
things where food is involved – To do last-minute
plans – So I don't feel as cold – Last-minute
sleepovers with friends – Because being skinnier
never actually made me happier.

What are yours?

RESOURCES

EATING DISORDER HELP – UK

- Anorexia Bulimia Care: if you are over 18 they offer a befriending scheme. www.anorexiabulimiacare.org.uk
- BEAT: provides online and phone support. www. beateatingdisorders.org.uk, Helpline: 0808 801 0677, Studentline: 0808 801 0811, Youthline: 0808 801 0711
- First Steps ED: a fantastic charity that focuses massively on early intervention, giving you a space to come and speak up. firststepsed.co.uk
- Freedfromed.co.uk: this is a network of NHS organizations offering early intervention support.
- Linda Tremble Foundation: www.lindatremblefoundation.org.uk
- Eating Disorder Association Northern Ireland: www. eatingdisordersni.co.uk
- The Laurence Trust: www.thelaurencetrust.co.uk
- NHS: www.nhs.uk/conditions/eating-disorders

EATING DISORDER HELP – GLOBAL

- Break Binge Eating: breakbingeeating.com
- Global Foundation for Eating Disorders (GFED): www.gfed.org
- International Eating Disorder Family Support (IEDFS) facebook group: www.facebook.com/groups/International.Eating. Disorder.Family.Support.IEDFS
- MentorCONNECT: mentorconnect-ed.org
- Diabetics with eating disorders: dwed.org.uk/global

EATING DISORDER HELP – US

- National Eating Disorders Association (NEDA): this organization has some brilliant blogs as well as a crisis text messenger service and helpline. www.nationaleatingdisorders.org
- Eating Disorder Hope: www.eatingdisorderhope.com/treatment-for-eating-disorders/international
- Project Heal (also found in Canada and Australia): www.theprojectheal.org
- Alliance for Eating Disorders: www.allianceforeatingdisorders.com
- National Association of Anorexia Nervosa and Associated Disorders (ANAD): anad.org

EATING DISORDER HELP – AUSTRALIA

- The Butterfly Foundation: butterfly.org.au

UK-BASED COURSES FOR EATING DISORDER RECOVERY

These 4-8-week courses allow people with eating disorders to explore certain areas further.

- Tastelife: www.tastelifeuk.org
- Keys To Freedom: www.mercyuk.org/keystofreedom (Christian discipleship)

SUPPORT FOR FAMILIES/CARERS

- FEAST: for parents and carers of those struggling. www.feast-ed.org
- New Maudsley Approach: specific advice for parents and carers. thenewmaudsleyapproach.co.uk
- YoungMinds: parent helpline 0808 8025544

MENTAL HEALTH SUPPORT

- Crisis Text Line: www.crisistextline.org, 24/7 crisis support UK text 85258
- Hub of Hope: provides a quick way to pull up a list of services in your area. It also has a crisis text message scheme just in case you need someone to talk to. hubofhope.co.uk
- Samaritans: www.samaritans.org, 24 hours, call 116 123
- Shout for support in a crisis: www.giveusashout.org, text 85258
- Mind: here you will find some really helpful worksheets. www.mind.org.uk
- Mind and Soul Foundation: www.mindandsoulfoundation.org
- The Mix: offers online support, as well as a heap of information. It is mainly for under 25-year-olds but there is a lot of great stuff on there! www.themix.org.uk
- YoungMinds: youngminds.org.uk

Please remember that reaching out for support is not weak, and you don't have to be at rock bottom to seek support.

STUDENT SUPPORT

- Student Minds: a huge hub of knowledge – have a look at their blogs and their support sections. www.studentminds.org.uk
- Student Space: set up by Student Minds, has a place for finding support, a place to reach out for support and blogs to read. studentspace.org.uk

FINDING A THERAPIST OR COUNSELLOR

- British Association for Counselling and Psychotherapy: www.bacp.co.uk/search/Therapists

ABOUT US

Welbeck Balance publishes books dedicated to changing lives. Our mission is to deliver life-enhancing books to help improve your wellbeing so that you can live your life with greater clarity and meaning, wherever you are on life's journey. Our Trigger books are specifically devoted to opening up conversations about mental health and wellbeing.

Welbeck Balance and Trigger are part of the Welbeck Publishing Group – a globally recognised independent publisher based in London. Welbeck are renowned for our innovative ideas, production values and developing long-lasting content. Our books have been translated into over 30 languages in more than 60 countries around the world.

Find out more at:
www.welbeckpublishing.com
Twitter.com/welbeckpublish
Instagram.com/welbeckpublish
Facebook.com/welbeckuk

Find out more about Trigger at:
www.triggerhub.org
Twitter.com/triggercalm
Instagram.com/triggercalm
Facebook.com/triggercalm

WELBECK
BALANCE